THE LUMINOUS MYSTERIES

THE LUMINOUS MYSTERIES
Biblical Reflections on the Life of Christ

TIM GRAY
FOREWORD BY ARCHBISHOP RAYMOND L. BURKE

EMMAUS
ROAD
PUBLISHING

Steubenville, Ohio
A Division of Catholics United for the Faith

Emmaus Road Publishing
827 North Fourth Street
Steubenville, Ohio 43952

Library of Congress Control Number: 2004109980
ISBN 1-931018-20-0

Cover design and layout by
Beth Hart

Cover artwork:
Michael O'Brien, *The Transfiguration*
www.studiobrien.com
Used with permission

Nihil Obstat: Rev. James Dunfee, *Censor Librorum*
Imprimatur: ✠ R. Daniel Conlon, D.D., J.C.D., Ph.D.
Bishop of Steubenville
Date: May 5, 2004

Lady, thou art so great and so powerful,
that whoever desires grace yet does not turn to thee,
would have his desire fly without wings.

—Dante

Contents

—I—
The First Luminous Mystery
The Baptism in the Jordan

—II—
The Second Luminous Mystery
The Wedding of Cana

—III—
The Third Luminous Mystery
The Proclamation of the Kingdom of God

—IV—
The Fourth Luminous Mystery
The Transfiguration

—VI—
The Fifth Luminous Mystery
The Institution of the Eucharist

Foreword

At the dawn of the third Christian millennium, our Holy Father Pope John Paul II has written to us on three matters relating to the heart of our life in Christ: the pastoral plan for the new evangelization (apostolic letter *Novo Millennio Ineunte*); the praying of the Rosary (apostolic letter *Rosarium Virginis Mariae*); and the Holy Eucharist (encyclical letter *Ecclesia de Eucharistia*). The teaching contained in these papal documents, which are closely related to each other by our Holy Father's express intention, focuses our attention on the heart of the new evangelization required in our time (*EE* 6)—namely, the teaching, celebrating, and living of the Gospel as if for the first time, with the energy and enthusiasm of the first disciples. It focuses our attention on Christ alive for us in the Church and our daily response of unconditional love to God's all-merciful love of us.

The apostolic letter *Rosarium Virginis Mariae*, the "Marian crowning" of the Holy Father's teaching at the dawn of the new Christian millennium (*EE* 6), invites us to uncover anew the simplicity and depth of this powerful prayer given to the Church in the first centuries of the second Christian millennium, "loved by countless saints and encouraged by the Magisterium" (*RVM* 1). The Holy Father, in a wonderful way, describes for us the nature of the Rosary—a drawing close to our Blessed Mother through prayer—in order that, with her, we may look upon the face of Christ and enter into conversation with Him who alone is our salvation. In describing the inspiration for writing this apostolic letter on the Rosary, our Holy Father states: "I have felt drawn to offer a reflection on the Rosary, as a kind of Marian complement to that letter [*Novo Millennio Ineunte*] and an exhortation to contemplate the Face of Christ in union with, and at the school of His Most Holy Mother" (*RVM* 3).

Contemplating the face of Christ is, at one and the same time, the contemplation of the mystery of our life in Christ, leading us to grow in Christ's likeness, to grow in holiness of life (cf. *RVM* 5).

This apostolic letter on the Rosary not only helps us to uncover anew the power of this beloved prayer for our daily conversion of life to Christ, but it also contains a wonderful gift for our deeper contemplation of Christ and of the mystery of our life in Him. Our Holy Father offers to us five new mysteries of the Rosary—the Mysteries of Light or Luminous Mysteries—in order that our contemplation of the face of Christ could "include *the mysteries of Christ's public ministry between His Baptism and His Passion*" (*RVM* 19). Taking his cue from the words of the Gospel, "While I am in the world, I am the light of the world" (Jn. 9:5), our Holy Father has named the new mysteries "The Luminous Mysteries." As the Holy Father observes, reflecting upon the public ministry of Jesus, beginning with His baptism in the Jordan and concluding with the celebration of the Last Supper—or more accurately, the Institution of the Holy Eucharist—we see how Christ sheds divine light upon every aspect of our being and of our world.

In a certain way, the Holy Father's gift of the Luminous Mysteries is inspired by the description of the Rosary given by Pope Pius XII and quoted by Pope Paul VI in his apostolic exhortation *Marialis Cultus*: "the compendium of the entire Gospel" (*RVM* 1, 19). The Luminous Mysteries permit our prayerful contemplation of the face of Christ and reflection upon our life in Christ to be more complete, to include the words and deeds of our Lord during His public ministry. The Holy Father, in a striking way, describes our spiritual life, our life of prayer and devotion, as the way to unite our poor hearts more completely to the Sacred Heart of Jesus (*RVM* 19). Clearly, all of the mysteries of the Rosary—Joyous, Luminous, Sorrowful, and Glorious—lead us to the heart of Jesus, to that font of immeasurable love. The mysteries of the Rosary lead us to God the Son who, through the overshadowing of the Holy Spirit, took a human heart under the Immaculate Heart of Mary, in order to save us from sin and everlasting death. Our Blessed Mother, who united her Immaculate Heart completely to the Sacred Heart of Jesus from the moment of the Incarnation, draws us to His glorious pierced Heart through the praying of the Holy Rosary.

Inspired by *Rosarium Virginis Mariae*, Tim Gray has prepared a series of meditations on the Luminous Mysteries— his own meditation and the meditation of one of the Fathers of the Church on the Word of God in which each mystery is revealed. His meditations, enriched by those of the Fathers of the Church, achieve the noble end for which he wrote them. They enrich our contemplation of the life of Christ and "thereby deepen [our] Rosary meditation."

Tim Gray is an outstanding teacher of the Catholic faith, as he has demonstrated by his other writings and his presentations given to a variety of audiences. His love of Christ is transparent in his writing and inspires the reader to love Christ more fully and ardently. *The Luminous Mysteries: Biblical Reflections on the Life of Christ* is a most worthy tool for growth in the knowledge of Christ and growth in Christ's likeness. It is a most worthy instrument for carrying out the new evangelization. It is my hope that his meditations will inspire the regular praying of the Rosary in all homes, so that they will become ever more the first place in which we come to know Christ and to live in Him. The new evangelization begun in the home will extend to our parishes and local communities, to our nation and our world.

May your study of these meditations on the Luminous Mysteries of the Rosary help you "to *contemplate with Mary the Face of Christ*" (*RVM* 3).

—MOST REV. RAYMOND L. BURKE
Archbishop of St. Louis
Memorial of Saint Elizabeth of Hungary, 2004

Abbreviations

Old Testament

Gen./Genesis
Ex./Exodus
Lev./Leviticus
Num./Numbers
Deut./Deuteronomy
Josh./Joshua
Judg./Judges
Ruth/Ruth
1 Sam./1 Samuel
2 Sam./2 Samuel
1 Kings/1 Kings
2 Kings/2 Kings
1 Chron./1 Chronicles
2 Chron./2 Chronicles
Ezra/Ezra
Neh./Nehemiah
Tob./Tobit
Jud./Judith
Esther/Esther
Job/Job
Ps./Psalms
Prov./Proverbs
Eccles./Ecclesiastes
Song/Song of Solomon
Wis./Wisdom
Sir./Sirach (Ecclesiasticus)
Is./Isaiah
Jer./Jeremiah
Lam./Lamentations
Bar./Baruch

Ezek./Ezekiel
Dan./Daniel
Hos./Hosea
Joel/Joel
Amos/Amos
Obad./Obadiah
Jon./Jonah
Mic./Micah
Nahum/Nahum
Hab./Habakkuk
Zeph./Zephaniah
Hag./Haggai
Zech./Zechariah
Mal./Malachi
1 Mac./1 Maccabees
2 Mac./2 Maccabees

New Testament

Mt./Matthew
Mk./Mark
Lk./Luke
Jn./John
Acts/Acts of the Apostles
Rom./Romans
1 Cor./1 Corinthians
2 Cor./2 Corinthians
Gal./Galatians
Eph./Ephesians
Phil./Philippians
Col./Colossians
1 Thess./1 Thessalonians

2 Thess./2 Thessalonians
1 Tim./1 Timothy
2 Tim./2 Timothy
Tit./Titus
Philem./Philemon
Heb./Hebrews
Jas./James
1 Pet./1 Peter

2 Pet./2 Peter
1 Jn./1 John
2 Jn./2 John
3 Jn./3 John
Jude/Jude
Rev./Revelation
(Apocalypse)

Introduction

A meditative praying of the Rosary should always be a life-giving encounter with Jesus Christ. This is particularly true for the Luminous Mysteries—the Mysteries of Light—which Pope John Paul II has bequeathed to humanity at the end of his pontificate. He has given them as a kind of last will and testament, the seasoned fruit of his deep devotion to Christ through Mary. The Pope's fervent desire in bringing forth the five new Mysteries of Light is to breathe "fresh life" into this ancient prayer and to "enkindle renewed interest in the Rosary's place within Christian spirituality."[1]

In giving us a new way of praying these ancient mysteries of Christ's life, the Pope has given us something from the depths of his heart—the love of Christ that has been his heart's desire, a love he fervently wants to share with all of us. For Pope John Paul II, the Rosary is a "true doorway to the depths of the Heart of Christ" (*RVM* 19). All we need to do is take up the beads and pray our way through that door.

The Pope calls the Rosary the "school of Mary." This does not mean, as those unacquainted with the Rosary may suppose, that Mary is the goal or object of this prayer. On the contrary, the "school of Mary" has for its entire curriculum and focus the person of Jesus Christ. Who spent more time looking upon Jesus than Mary, as she

---

[1] Pope John Paul II, Apostolic Letter on the Most Holy Rosary *Rosarium Virginis Mariae* (October 16, 2002), no. 19 (hereafter cited in text as *RVM*).

watched her beloved child slowly grow into a strong young man? Who spoke to Jesus more than Mary? Who was present with Him more than anyone else? Who modeled trust and faith in Jesus more than Mary? The Holy Father tells us: "As we contemplate each mystery of her Son's life, she invites us to do as she did at the Annunciation: to ask humbly the questions which open us to the light, in order to end with the obedience of faith: 'Behold I am the hand-maid of the Lord; be it done to me according to your word' (Lk. 1:38)" (*RVM* 14). By taking up this Marian prayer, we are, in a sense, transported to Mary's side, so that like her, we too can "contemplate the beauty on the face of Christ and . . . experience the depths of his love" (*RVM* 1).

The Pope observes that "families seldom manage to come together, and the rare occasions when they do are often taken up with watching television. To return to the recitation of the family Rosary means filling daily life with very different images, images of the mystery of salvation: the image of the Redeemer, the image of his most Blessed Mother" (*RVM* 41). The number of images that we take in through modern technology is legion. Long ago, Paul warned Christians not to be "conformed to this world but be transformed by the renewal of your mind" (Rom. 12:2). How do we go about being transformed in Christ? There is simply no other way than prayer. By taking up the Rosary and filling our minds with the mysteries of Christ's life, we put into action Paul's admonition to set our minds "on things that are above, not on things that are on earth" (Col. 3:2). We who were made in God's image and likeness cannot allow our lives to be painted after the images of the world. But this takes our cooperation. The Holy Spirit, the Divine Iconographer, can paint the image of Christ on our souls only when we are open to Him in the stillness of prayer.

Much of Mary's contemplation, especially later in life, was the fruit of her remembering. *Remembering* is a vital word and concept in Scripture: "We need to understand this word in the biblical sense of remembrance (*zakar*) as a making present of the works brought about by God in the history of salvation" (*RVM* 13). Every time we pray the mysteries of the Rosary, we recall and remember the mysteries of Jesus' life, death, and Resurrection—opening us to the grace that Christ won for us. Reflecting on the mysteries of Christ's life in our mind and in our heart can profoundly assimilate us into the image of Christ. The bottom line is that we are creatures of imitation. The question is, then: Will we let our lives be shaped by Hollywood, or by the holy images of the Gospel?

The Torah of Israel emphasized the vital importance of memory (*zakar*) for God's people. They were encouraged to constantly "remember all the way which the LORD your God has led you," while at the same time warned not to "forget" the Lord, especially when surrounded by comfort and affluence (cf. Deut. 8). Our ability of remembering is completely dependent on how often we pray. Pray seldom, and you will seldom remember God. This is one of the secrets of the Rosary; it keeps the memory of Christ fresh in our hearts. Constant meditation on the life of Christ, such as the Rosary offers us, will "deepen our convictions of faith, prompt the conversion of our heart, and strengthen our will to follow Christ" (*Catechism*, no. 2708).

The Luminous Mysteries are a "compendium of the Gospel" (*RVM* 19), as the Pope puts it, and that is why they are my favorite set of mysteries of the Rosary. In this simple book, I have set forward some reflections on the biblical foundation of the Mysteries of Light: our Lord's Baptism in the Jordan, the Wedding Feast of Cana, the Proclamation of the Kingdom, the Transfiguration of our Lord, and finally, the Institution of the Eucharist. Also, drawing on the richness of Catholic Tradition, I have included excerpts from the writings of four Church Fathers. As Scripture says, "Every scribe . . . brings out of his treasure what is new and what is old" (Mt. 13:53).

My hope is that this book will enrich your "memories" and images of Christ's life, and thereby deepen your Rosary meditation. Christ is the light of the world, and that light can chase away the many shadows that encroach upon our hearts today. I promise you that studying God's Word will bring astonishing light to your heart and life, as King David recognized long ago: "The unfolding of thy words gives light" (Ps. 119:130).

The First Luminous Mystery

The Baptism in the Jordan

The Baptism in the Jordan is first of all a mystery of light. Here, as Christ descends into the waters, the innocent one who became "sin" for our sake (cf. 2 Cor. 5:21), the heavens open wide and the voice of the Father declares him the beloved Son (cf. Mt. 3:17 and parallels), while the Spirit descends on him to invest him with the mission which he is to carry out.

—*John Paul II,* Rosarium Virginis Mariae

"This Is My Beloved Son"

Then Jesus came from Galilee to the Jordan to John, to be baptized by him. John would have prevented him, saying, "I need to be baptized by you, and do you come to me?" But Jesus answered him, "Let it be so now; for thus it is fitting for us to fulfil all righteousness." Then he consented. And when Jesus was baptized, he went up immediately from the water, and behold, the heavens were opened and he saw the Spirit of God descending like a dove, and alighting on him; and lo, a voice from heaven, saying, "This is my beloved Son, with whom I am well pleased." (Mt. 3:13–17)[1]

It is often thought that the baptism of Jesus held no real significance for His mission and life. Instead it is suggested that He submitted to baptism simply out of humility, and to associate Himself with a rite that would later be important for Christian initiation. However, if we look at its context, we see there is much more to Jesus' baptism than a ritual washing. Israel was being summoned by the

---

[1] See also Mk. 1:9–11; Lk. 3:21–22.

Prophet John to come for baptism at the Jordan River, to confess their sins and repent. Of course, Jesus, being sinless, had nothing to confess. John himself recognized this immediately, for Matthew tells us that when Jesus submitted to John and his washing, "John would have prevented him, saying, 'I need to be baptized by you, and do you come to me?" (Mt. 3:14).

Why, then, did Jesus journey to the Jordan in order to appear before the prophet, especially when He did not need to confess and wash? The problem is acute for us—for if Jesus' journey to the Jordan holds little meaning, then why should we bother to join Jesus at the Jordan through the journey of meditation? In short, was Jesus only going through the motions of a prophetic rite in order to give us a pious model, or is there a rich mystery for meditation in Jesus' baptism?

The answer, of course, is that there is more in this event than a demonstration of humility and a model for piety—the baptism of Jesus profoundly impacted the cosmos, and Jesus' own mission, in many ways. Indeed, Jesus' baptism is so rich a mystery that a lifetime of meditation could never exhaust its meaning.

"Then Jesus Came from Galilee to the Jordan"

We must begin with the Jordan River, since Providence chose this place as the setting for Jesus' baptism. The Jordan River begins north the Promised Land, near the heights of Mount Hermon in eastern Lebanon. Descending from these heights, the river flows into the northern portion of the Sea of Galilee. From the southern part of the sea, it continues its descent through

the Jordan valley until it reaches its terminus at the low-
est place in all the earth, the Dead Sea. The river's two
hundred-mile winding descent to the Dead Sea is the
basis of its name in Hebrew, *yar-dane*, which means
"descender." It is here, at the river named "Descender,"
that a drop more dramatic than the 2,380 foot descent of
the Jordan River will occur, for it is here that the heavens
will be opened and the Holy Spirit will descend upon
Jesus. The River Jordan is bound to the mystery of
descent—the descent of waters that will refresh and give
life to God's children.

Israel first encountered the Jordan when Joshua led the
people out of the wilderness. The day the people of Israel
came to the eastern side of the Jordan, Joshua declared:
"Sanctify yourselves; for tomorrow the LORD will do won-
ders among you" (Josh. 3:5). The next day, Joshua
instructed the priests to lead the people across the river,
carrying the ark of the covenant. When the priests brought
the ark into the river, the waters stopped flowing, allowing
the people to cross, dry-shod, into the Promised Land.
With this, the Jordan River came to symbolize for Israel
the end of the desert wanderings and the entry into the
long-awaited Promised Land.

Later in Israel's history, God called the Prophet Elijah
to the Jordan River. Elijah and his assistant, Elisha, came
down from the north, traveling through Gilgal, Bethel,
and finally Jericho, to approximately the same area where
Joshua led Israel into the Promised Land (2 Kings 2:1–5).
They then crossed out of the Promised Land to the eastern side of the Jordan by the miraculous action of Elijah,
who parted the waters in a manner reminiscent of Joshua's

5

crossing (2 Kings 2:8). The difference, however, was the direction in which they crossed. Elijah crossed out of the land, eastward, whereas Joshua crossed westward, entering into the Promised Land. Joshua's mission was one of entering; Elijah's one of exiting.

Elijah knew that he had been led to the Jordan because his time had come to leave the land and the people of Israel. As he stood on the banks of the river with Elisha, a fiery chariot swung down to earth, taking Elijah in a whirlwind up to heaven. But Elisha was not left behind empty-handed. He inherited the mantle of Elijah and a double portion of his spirit (2 Kings 2:6–14). Elijah had been the mightiest of the prophets, but now his successor, Elisha, would wield even more power in the Spirit of the Lord—healing lepers, multiplying bread to feed a multitude, and even raising the dead. Once again, the Jordan is a place of transition. This time, it marks the end of one prophet's mission and the beginning of another—a transition marked by the bestowal of the Spirit and the opening of heaven.

"To the Jordan to John"

Why did John summon all of Israel to come out of their villages and cities in order to walk through the wilderness of Judea to the Jordan River? Certainly John could have held his ritual washing in Jerusalem. There were plenty of cisterns and pools for ritual washing near the Temple. Indeed, what better place for ritual washing and repentance than the city that held Mount Zion and the Temple? Where better than the Temple, for that matter, to confess sins and seek forgiveness?

The Jews were certainly a people with a strong sense of geography. This is illustrated by the fact that their Scriptures focus so much on one particular piece of real estate—the Promised Land. In that land, no place was more holy than the Temple, so the question is worth raising: why did the Prophet John make the Jordan River the base of his preaching and ministry?

As we have already seen, the Jordan was a place that held certain national memories, the foremost being the entry into the Promised Land and its conquest by Joshua. Since John is eventually arrested by Herod, it is likely that John operated on the eastern side of the Jordan; that is, outside of the strict boundary of the Promised Land. We know this because Herod controlled the land of Galilee in the north and the land east of the Jordan. The land on the west side of the Jordan (and in the Promised Land), in the area of Judea, was controlled directly by the Romans, specifically by Pontius Pilate. Therefore, the fact that Herod had John arrested points to the strong probability that John was based on the east side of the river—the only side over which Herod had jurisdiction.

Thus John had the people of Israel cross the Jordan eastward to hear his preaching and instructions. He called Israel out of the Promised Land to repent and be ritually baptized. Then, after they had been baptized in the river, they would cross westward, back into the Promised Land (as their forefathers had done with Joshua). The point was obvious: Israel needed to repent and be cleansed of her sins, and to start over. John was inviting Israel to begin afresh as the people of God, to go back to their land and homes with a renewed relationship with Him.

In the midst of this prophetic reentry, a man of God named "Joshua" showed up—that is, Jesus (the name "Jesus" in Hebrew is literally "Joshua"). John himself had said that he was just the precursor to someone greater who was to follow—someone who would baptize not simply with water, but with the Holy Spirit. Jesus' appearance at the Jordan is quickly recognized by John as the coming, not of some simple pilgrim, but of one "whose sandals I am not worthy to carry" (Mt. 3:11). Jesus instructs John to baptize Him, and as he does so, the Holy Spirit descends from heaven and rests on Jesus.

The presence of two prophets at the Jordan is again reminiscent of the story of Elijah and Elisha. It was at the Jordan that the prophetic "baton" was passed between the two men of God and the successor received a more powerful share of the Spirit. Thus, "those who have ears to hear" can discern the story of Elijah replayed at a new level. John plays Elijah to Jesus' Elisha—for when John anoints Jesus, "the Spirit of God descend[s] like a dove" (Mt. 3:16). Like Elisha, Jesus will exercise a ministry greater than that of His predecessor. In both stories, the Jordan is the locus of the transition of mission and the giving of the Spirit.

Are we to believe, then, that John is a new Elijah? Certainly Jesus held John to be a type of Elijah, for He said, "[I]f you are willing to accept it, he is Elijah who is to come" (Mt. 11:14). This strange reference to Elijah's return is a reference to the last prophetic oracle given to Israel, which came from the Prophet Malachi. Malachi's last word to Israel was that Elijah would come to visit the people before the Lord's own advent (see Mal. 4:5). Thus Jesus, by proclaiming John to be the new Elijah, was suggesting that the day of the Lord was at hand—they should be on the lookout for His appearance.

Undoubtedly, many of the Jews of John's day did in fact see him as the new Elijah. John certainly dressed the part. His wardrobe of a leather belt and garment of camel's hair was strikingly similar to how Elijah dressed (2 Kings 1:8). It is also worth observing that Elijah was a prophet who upset the ruling king of Israel, Ahab, and his wicked wife, Jezebel. Similarly, John boldly spoke out against King Herod and incurred the wrath of his wicked queen, Herodias—the new Jezebel. The story of Israel's past was being replayed in a different but familiar key.

Just as John is reminiscent of Elijah, so too are there parallels between Jesus and Elisha. Elisha's mission began with the bestowal of God's Spirit; Jesus also received an outpouring of the Spirit at the Jordan. And this emerging pattern continues. For just as Elisha, anointed in the power of God's Spirit, went forth and cured a leper, multiplied bread, and even raised the dead, so too will the new "Elisha"—Jesus.

The Jordan is a conduit of more than water. It connects back to the stories of Israel's entry into the Promised Land with Joshua, back to Israel's spiritual crisis and call for renewal with Elijah and Elisha. By reflecting on the significance of the Jordan in Israel's history, we can come to appreciate the rich meaning that it holds for John's baptism of Jesus. Jesus is not simply going through the motions of a Jewish ritual when He allows John to baptize Him. Rather, in Jesus, the New Israel, the story of Israel is repeated at a deeper level and brought to a prophetic climax. Now the real Joshua has come to set His people free. The greater "Elisha," now anointed, is about to begin a prophetic ministry that will unleash the power of the Spirit like none other.

"And When Jesus Was Baptized"

The arrival of a prophet at the Jordan, after many generations of prophetic drought (remember, the last prophet was Malachi, who ministered several hundred years before Jesus), caused no small stir among the people. The question quickly arose: Could this be the Messiah? With the multitudes streaming out of Jerusalem to be baptized by this new prophet, the leaders in Jerusalem wasted no time in dispatching a team of priests and Levites to investigate. But John confessed to them, "I am not the Christ" (Jn. 1:20).

What did John and the Jewish people mean by the title "Christ"? The word "christ" is the Greek word for the Hebrew "messiah." In both languages, they literally mean "one who is anointed." In the ancient kingdom of Israel, kings were anointed with oil, marking their ordination to the royal office.

For example, the Prophet Samuel anointed the first king, Saul: "Then Samuel took a vial of oil and poured it on his head, and kissed him and said, 'Has not the LORD anointed you to be prince over his people Israel?'" (1 Sam. 10:1). Notice the sacramental nature of the act. The prophet pours the oil on Saul, but it is the Lord who anoints him king. The anointing of Saul is then followed by the Spirit coming mightily upon him and transforming him. Samuel tells the newly anointed king: "[T]he spirit of the LORD will come mightily upon you, and you shall prophesy with them and be turned into another man" (1 Sam. 10:6).

Later, God tells Samuel to anoint a new king from among the sons of Jesse. Samuel, led by God, anoints the youngest of Jesse's sons, David: "Then Samuel took the horn of oil, and anointed him in the midst of his brothers; and the Spirit of the LORD came mightily upon David from that day forward" (1 Sam. 16:13). The office of king was so important and sacred that it required anointing by a prophet. This anointing not only bestows the office of king, but also the gift of the Holy Spirit.

Thus, when John is asked if he is the "Christ," the issue at hand is kingship. John demurs, saying, "After me comes he who is mightier than I" (Mk. 1:7). It is then that Jesus, in order to present Himself to be anointed king over Israel, comes down from Galilee to be baptized by John. The mightier one has come!

"And He Saw the Spirit of God Descending like a Dove"

After Jesus submitted to John's baptism, He "went up immediately from the water, and behold, the heavens were opened and he saw the Spirit of God descending like a dove" (Mt. 3:16). Every Gospel account of Jesus' baptism focuses on the descent of the Holy Spirit upon Jesus. As the Spirit had come upon Saul and David when the prophet anointed them, so too the power of the Holy Spirit descends upon Jesus as He comes to the prophet at the Jordan. From this moment onward, Jesus can be called "Christ."

After the descent of the Holy Spirit upon Jesus, a voice from heaven declares, "Thou art my beloved Son; with thee I am well pleased" (Lk. 3:22). This declaration from the Father is worded so as to echo an important royal psalm that was used for the enthronement of the Davidic kings.

Psalm 2 begins by observing that the kings and leaders of the nations conspire against the Lord and His "anointed" (Ps. 2:1–2). But the Lord responds to their schemes with laughter and confirms the status of His anointed one, saying, "I have set my king on Zion, my holy hill" (v. 6). Then the anointed one responds, saying, "I will tell of the decree of the Lord: He said to me, 'You are my son, today I have begotten you'" (v. 7). Note that "anointed one," as we saw earlier, is synonymous with "king." The king in Israel would have had this psalm read during his enthronement ceremony, at which he was anointed king and, therefore, adopted son to the Lord. Thus the declaration by the Father Himself, with the words of the royal enthronement psalm, strongly suggests that Jesus' baptism was the occasion at which He was anointed for His royal mission.

The descent of the Holy Spirit, the presentation before the prophet, and the echoes of a royal enthronement psalm all point to the conclusion that there is more to Jesus' baptism than a ritual washing; rather, it is the occasion of Jesus' royal anointing. Jesus, in His divine nature, is always and eternally the only begotten Son of the Father. In His human nature, taken from Mary, Jesus was born into the line of David; so, like all the Davidic kings, He too must be anointed at a particular time and place. The Evangelist Luke understands that time and place to be Jesus' baptism at the Jordan.

Unlike Matthew, who begins the story of Jesus with His genealogy, Luke waits until the end of chapter 3, immediately after the account of Jesus' baptism, to list His geneology. Why does Luke put it off until this precise moment? The answer is simple: Luke holds that the baptism of Jesus is the occasion at which He is anointed the "Christ." The genealogy reveals that Jesus is of the line of David (Lk. 3:31), which validates the previous baptism account that made Jesus King.

Luke also stresses that Jesus was anointed in the Spirit. Although the term "anointed" is not used in the baptism narrative, the fact that the Holy Spirit descends on Jesus suffices, as anointing bestows the Spirit for the sake of faithfully living out the holy office to which one is ordained. Indeed, in the very next chapter, Luke tells us that Jesus went forth "full of the Holy Spirit" (Lk. 4:1), much like David after his anointing, when "the Spirit of the Lord came mightily" upon him (1 Sam. 16:13).

Also in the same chapter, following the baptism, Jesus begins His first public proclamation with the words of Isaiah, declaring: "The Spirit of the Lord is upon me, because he has anointed me to preach good news to the poor" (Lk. 4:18; cf. Is. 61:1–2). Note that Jesus claims the Spirit is upon Him because He has been "anointed." Thus, Luke clearly shows us that Jesus interprets His baptism as an anointing in the Spirit—an anointing that sends Jesus forth on His royal messianic mission.

Who anointed Jesus, John or God? In one sense, the answer is both. Recall the story of Samuel anointing Saul (see 1 Sam. 10:1). The narrator tells us that Samuel anointed him with oil, but then Samuel tells Saul that *God* has anointed him king. The prophet acts on God's behalf. But in the baptism of Jesus there is no oil; instead of this sign, there is the reality to which it points—the Holy Spirit—seen in the form of a dove. The Father declares His love for the Son, and so, here too God's involvement is uniquely evident.

Luke subtly but carefully shows us that Jesus' baptism is the profound event wherein God the Father anoints Jesus for His royal messianic mission. Luke makes this clear in Acts 10, where he records Peter preaching a homily at the first baptism of Gentiles. In the homily, Peter explains how everything started with John's preaching a baptism and "how God anointed Jesus of Nazareth with the Holy Spirit and with power" (Acts 10:38). Jesus did not come to the Jordan and to John to be washed of sin; rather, He came to Israel's last prophet to be anointed the final and everlasting King.

"And Behold, the Heavens Were Opened"

Amidst the oracles of hope and prophecies of restoration that dominate the second half of Isaiah, a rare complaint arises against God. The prophet laments over the absence of God among His people and expresses this with deep longing for the Lord to reveal Himself once again. "Where is he who put in the midst of them his holy Spirit?" (Is. 63:11). As fire brings water to boil, so too these cries to God, who seems absent, kindle a complaint that becomes a lament. At the climax of the lament, he cries out, "O that thou wouldst rend the heavens and come down, that the mountains might quake at thy presence" (Is. 64:1). The imagery of quaking mountains evokes the most memorable manifestation of God, the theophany of Sinai.

The plight of Israel during the several hundred years of exile and domination under pagan rule only sharpened the desire for God's presence and intervention in the life of Israel: how long until the Lord rends the heavens and comes down? The Evangelist Mark gives Israel the answer.

Both Matthew and Luke describe the descent of the Holy Spirit upon Jesus as beginning with the opening up of the heavens. However, Mark's description, although consonant with these accounts, is more graphic. Instead of narrating that the heavens simply "opened up," Mark tells us that they were "rent open" (Mk. 1:10)—that is, they were violently torn. The Greek word employed by Mark is *schidzo*, from which we get the word "schism," which means "tearing apart." Thus, for Mark, the baptism of Jesus impacted the cosmos in such a powerful way that the heavens were torn open.

Jesus' baptism changed the world by rending open the heavens, allowing the Holy Spirit to descend in a powerful way. God finally heeded the lament lodged at the end of Isaiah: He rent the heavens and came down. The descent of the Spirit on Jesus—the advent of a new theophany like Sinai—marks the fulfillment of this desire for God's return. On Sinai, God revealed His Law to Moses; now, His New Law is not given on stony tablets, but is the Holy Spirit Himself, given through Jesus.

The Torah, or Law, was the light of Israel, as illustrated in the words of Psalm 119, which famously celebrates the Torah, saying, "Thy word is a lamp to my feet, and a light to my path" (Ps. 119:105). But now there is a new revelation—God manifests Himself no longer through stone, but through His Son. Jesus, with the anointing presence of the

Holy Spirit, represents the New Law of the New Covenant. Thus He can say, "I am the light of the world; he who follows me will not walk in darkness, but will have the light of life" (Jn. 8:12). Before, Israel had to walk by the light of the written Torah, but now they are called to walk in the light of Christ. The baptism of Jesus is the time that the light begins to dawn, as the clouds of heaven are rent for the descent of the Holy Spirit, who shines down upon the Son.

The striking image of tearing, *schidzo*, is found only one other time in Mark's Gospel. When Jesus utters a loud cry from the Cross and breathes His last, the curtain of the Temple is torn in two, from top to bottom (Mk. 15:38). The tearing of the heavens at the outset of Jesus' ministry is matched at its end with the tearing of the curtain that veiled the Holy of Holies in the Temple. This curtain stood as a barrier between the people and the Spirit of God, who resided in the Holy of Holies—where the ark of the covenant had been in Solomon's temple. Only the high priest, once a year, could go beyond the curtain into the inner sanctum of the Temple. With Jesus' death, the curtain is torn—signifying that access to the Holy Spirit is now open to all.

Why does Mark juxtapose the tearing of the heavens at Jesus' baptism with the tearing of the Temple curtain at Jesus' death? Is there a relationship between the baptism and death of Jesus? What is Mark suggesting by paralleling the heavens with the curtain that veils the Holy of Holies?

Certainly, the tearing open of the heavens at the baptism and the tearing of the Temple veil at the Cross signify the tearing down of the walls or barriers that had separated heaven and earth, God and His people. The parallel between the baptism of Jesus and the Paschal Mystery of His death is a suggestive and rich one, and one that Mark certainly intends. In the middle of his Gospel, Mark tells us of the time that James and John requested to sit at the right and left of Jesus when He comes into His glory. Jesus responds by asking if they can drink the cup He must drink, or be "baptized with the baptism with which I am baptized" (Mk. 10:38). Jesus' words are cryptic and strange. What is the baptism with which He will be baptized? These ominous words surely imply suffering. But has not Jesus already been baptized by John? Why then speak of another baptism? The answer, as Mark subtly shows us, is that Jesus' baptism in the Jordan already anticipated the ultimate baptism in His own blood on the Cross. Likewise, the Cross completes what was begun at the baptism. For Mark, the meaning of Jesus' baptism, and ours as well, can never be separated from the Paschal Mystery that is manifest on the Cross.

Few have penetrated the mystery of this relationship between Jesus' baptism and death as deeply as the Apostle Paul. He reminds the Christians in Rome how the Paschal Mystery defines Baptism: "Do you not know that all of us who have been baptized into Christ Jesus were baptized into his death? We were buried therefore with him by baptism into death, so that as Christ was raised from the dead by the glory of the Father, we too might walk in newness of life" (Rom. 6:3–4). Baptism, through the physical immersion under water, signifies death. The water of Baptism enters us into the death of Jesus, and we are "buried" with Him. But if going down into the water signifies death, then coming up out of the waters signifies rising with Christ, through a rebirth in the Spirit. Thus, the waters that symbolize death by drowning also signify rebirth and a new life.

Christian Baptism, therefore, is a ritual death and rebirth. It is, in other words, a sacramental entering into the Paschal Mystery—the death and Resurrection of Christ. We die to our old, fallen nature and sin, and rise to new life in Christ. Paul is adamant that the difference between the old and the new life is the indwelling of the Holy Spirit that begins at our baptism (cf. Rom. 8). With the bestowal of the Holy Spirit (remember, that is the focus of Jesus' baptism), we are not only endowed with the Spirit, but, even more, we are adopted as sons or daughters of our Heavenly Father. "[A]ll who are led by the Spirit of God are sons of God," and thus, at Baptism, one receives the "spirit of sonship" (Rom. 8:14–15).

When Jesus was baptized, the Holy Spirit manifestly descended upon Him, and the Father recognized Jesus' eternal sonship by declaring, "[T]hou art my beloved Son." The gift of the Spirit did not bestow sonship on Jesus, for He was already the eternal Son of the Father. Instead, the descent of the Spirit manifests what was already true of Jesus' relationship with the Father. And as we have already seen, the anointing in the Spirit gave to Jesus in His humanity the royal anointing of the Davidic kings of Israel, of whom He was heir. The beauty in receiving the Spirit at our baptism is that now we too become heirs. "When we cry, 'Abba! Father!' it is the Spirit himself bearing witness with our spirit that we are children of God, and if children, then heirs, heirs of God and fellow heirs with Christ, provided we suffer with him in order that we may also be glorified with him" (Rom. 8:15–17).

The bestowal of sonship through our baptism is an awesome mystery. The gift of the Holy Spirit, which Paul refers to as the Spirit of sonship, brings about a new creation in us at baptism. No wonder the heavens were torn asunder, and the Temple veil rent. For by His life and death, Jesus "has broken down the dividing wall . . . for through him we both have access in one Spirit to the Father" (Eph. 2:14, 18). The mystery of Jesus' sonship, manifest at His baptism, points to the mystery of our adopted sonship through the same Spirit. Thus, to reflect on the mystery and identity of Jesus at His baptism is to reflect on our own identity as well.

At Jesus' baptism, as we have seen, He is anointed the Christ—the Lord's Anointed One. At our baptism, we also are anointed with the Holy Spirit, and this too marks our identity. We are not called Christians simply because we try to follow Christ, but rather we are called Christians because we are anointed ones. We are anointed with God's Holy Spirit at baptism so that we can be empowered by the grace of the Spirit to follow Jesus. The mystery of Jesus' baptism contains profound light—not just to find our way, but moreover, to find our identity in Christ—so that we too can cry out daily, "Abba! Father!"

* * * *

Let us pray for the fruit of a deeper filial identity.
As we contemplate the mystery of Jesus' divine sonship in the mystery of His baptism, we pray for a deeper awareness of the adoption we received at our own baptism, when we became sons or daughters of our Father in Heaven. May the fruit of this mystery aid us in dying to sin and in living to holiness and the life of grace. Amen.

Points for Reflection

1. Just as the Jews saw that the Word of God (the Torah) was a light to their path (see Ps. 119:105), so now the path for the journey of our lives is to be illuminated by Christ. What does this mean for you practically in your life? How can you allow the light of Christ to shine on your life and help you to see the way that you should go? How can you share this light of Christ with others that you meet on your path?

2. Imagine the scene of Jesus' baptism: the heavens are rent open, the Spirit descends upon Jesus, and a voice calls out from heaven. It must have been a pretty amazing sight! Reflect upon your own baptism. Even though you probably didn't see the Holy Spirit come down as a dove, you now have the gift of the Spirit. How does this affect your relationship with God? How does this affect the way that you live? Are you connected to the Holy Spirit? How can the Holy Spirit play a greater role in your life?

3. Even though you did not physically hear the voice of the Father at your baptism, He really did say to you: "This is my beloved son," or, "This is my beloved daughter." Do you believe that you are a son or daughter of our loving Father in heaven? Do you have confidence in the fact that you are a son/daughter of God? Or are you insecure in this love, doubting that you truly are a beloved child? Imagine God the Father saying to you: "You are my beloved daughter," or, "You are my beloved son."

4. In our baptism, we are anointed as Christians. This means that we are followers of Christ. Just as Christ faced the Cross and embraced it, we too will have suffering and crosses in our lives. What are some of the crosses in your life? What is your first reaction to these sufferings and crosses? Do you often struggle to see where God is in the midst of suffering? Pray for the grace to see Jesus in the crosses in your life, and ask Him to be with you through them.

5. How did Jesus handle His suffering? What can you learn from Jesus' example, so that you can better deal with the crosses in your own life?

6. In Romans 6, Saint Paul says that we die to our fallen, sinful nature and rise to new life in Christ. Romans 6:11 says: "So you also must consider yourselves dead to sin and alive to God in Christ Jesus." How are we to continue to bury sin in our lives? Make a specific resolution to die to sin in your life (for example, go to Confession, pray for God's grace in a certain area of sin, ask someone to hold you accountable for a specific sin, make an examination of conscience, etc.)

Saint Hippolytus

All the works of our God and Savior are good—all of them that eye sees and mind perceives, all that reason interprets and hand touches, all that intellect comprehends and human nature understands. For what richer beauty can there be than that of the vast expanse of the sky? And what is fairer than the earth in bloom? And what more comforting than the seasonal winds? And what work more magnificent than the mosaic of the stars? And what brighter vision than the light of day? And what creature more excellent than man? Very good, indeed, are all the works of our God and Savior.

And what gift is more essential to life than water? For with water, all things are washed and nourished; all things are cleansed and bedewed. Water brings fruit to the earth. Water quickens the growing vine; it ripens the grape

"Reflections from the Fathers: Saint Hippolytus" is an adaptation of selections from "The Discourse on the Holy Theophany," in "The Extant Works and Fragments of Hippolytus: Part II, Dogmatical and Historical," *Ante-Nicene Fathers*, vol. 5; available from www.ccel.org. Adapted from the 1888 edition, Christian Literature Publishing.

cluster, softens the olive, and sweetens the palm-date. Water reddens the rose and decks the violet; it makes the lily bloom with its brilliant cups. Without the element of water, the present order of things cannot subsist.

This is not the only thing that proves the dignity of water. There is also that which is most honorable of all—the fact that Christ, the Maker of all, came down as the rain (Hos. 6:3), was known as a spring (Jn. 4:14), diffused Himself as a river (Jn. 7:38), and was baptized in the Jordan (Mt. 3:13). For you have heard how Jesus came to John and was baptized by him in the Jordan. Is it not strange, and wonderful beyond compare, that the boundless River (cf. Ps. 46:4), Jesus, who makes glad the city of God, should have been dipped in a little water? The illimitable Spring that bears life to all men, and has no end, was covered by poor and temporary waters! He who is present everywhere and absent nowhere—who is incomprehensible to angels and invisible to men—comes to the baptism of His own free will. When you hear these things, beloved, take them not only as spoken literally, but also accept them figuratively. Even the water took note of the kindness of the Lord's condescension to man. For, "when the waters saw thee, they were afraid" (Ps. 77:16). The waters of the river nearly overflowed their banks. Hence the prophet, having this in his view many generations ago, put the question, "What ails you, O sea, that you flee? O Jordan, that you turn back?" (Ps. 114:5). And the water said in reply, "We have seen the Creator of all things in the 'form of a servant' (cf. Phil 2:7), and being ignorant of the meaning of this mystery, we trembled with fear."

But we who know the meaning adore His mercy because He came to save and not to judge the world. John, the forerunner of the Lord, who did not know of this mystery beforehand, on learning that Jesus is truly Lord, cried out to those who came to be baptized by him, "You brood of vipers! Who warned you to flee from the wrath to come?" (Mt. 3:7). John told them, "I am not the Christ" (Jn. 1:20). "I am the servant, and not the lord; I am the subject, and not the king; I am the sheep, and not the shepherd; I am a man, and not God. By my birth I loosed the barrenness of my mother. I am a mere man; I did not come down from above. I bound the tongue of my father (cf. Lk. 1:20); I did not unfold divine grace. I am worthless, and the least; but 'among you stands one whom you do not know, even he who comes after me' (Jn. 1:27)—after me, indeed, in time, but before me by reason of the inaccessible and unutterable light of divinity. '[H]e who is coming after me is mightier than I, whose sandals I am not worthy to carry; he will baptize you with the Holy Spirit and with fire' (Mt. 3:11). I am subject to authority, but He has authority in Himself. I am bound by sins, but He is the Remover of sins. I apply the law, but He brings grace to light. I teach as a slave, but He judges as the Master. I have the earth as my dwelling, but He possesses heaven. I baptize with the baptism of repentance, but He confers the gift of adoption: 'He will baptize you with the Holy Spirit and with fire.' So why do you give attention to me? I am not the Christ."

As John says these things to the multitude, and as the people watch, hoping to see some strange spectacle, behold, the Lord appears—plain, solitary, and without escort. And not only did Jesus, as Lord without royal retinue, approach John, but like a mere man and one involved in sin, He bent His head to be baptized by the prophet. Upon seeing Jesus humble Himself so greatly, John was struck with astonishment at His action and tried to prevent Him, saying, "'I need to be baptized by you, and do you come to me?' (Mt. 3:14). "What are you doing, Lord? I have preached one thing (regarding You), and You perform another; the devil has heard one thing, and now perceives another. Baptize me with the fire of Your divinity; why do You wait upon water? Enlighten me with the Spirit; why do You submit to me, a creature? Baptize me, the Baptist, that Your preeminence may be known. I, Lord, baptize with the baptism of repentance, and I cannot baptize those who come to me unless they first confess fully their sins. How could it be, then, that I would baptize You? What do You have to confess? You are the Remover of sins; will You then be baptized with the baptism of repentance? Even if I should venture to baptize You, the Jordan River dares not come near You. 'I need to be baptized by you, and do you come to me?'"

And what does the Lord say to John? "'Let it be so now; for thus it is fitting for us to fulfill all righteousness' (Mt. 3:15). 'Let it be so now,' John; you are not wiser than I. You see as man; I foreknow as God. It is fitting for Me to do this first, and thus to teach. I engage in nothing unbecoming, for I am invested with honor. Do you marvel, John, that I have not come displaying my dignity? The purple robe of kings does not suit one in private station. Military splendor suits a king; am I coming to a prince, or to a friend? 'Let it be so now; for thus it is fitting for us to fulfill all righteousness.' I am the Fulfiller of the Law; I seek to fulfill it in its entirety, that after Me, Paul may exclaim, 'For Christ is the end of the law, that everyone who has faith may be justified' (Rom. 10:4). Baptize Me, John, in order that no one may despise baptism. I am baptized by you, the servant, so that no one among kings or dignitaries may scorn to be baptized by the hand of a poor priest. Let Me go down into the Jordan, so that they may hear My Father's testimony and recognize the power of the Son. 'Let it be so now; for thus it is fitting for us to fulfill all righteousness.'"

And at length, John bows to His will. "And when Jesus was baptized, he went immediately up from the water, and behold the heavens were opened and he saw the Spirit of God descending like a dove, and alighting on him; and lo, a voice from heaven, saying, "This is my beloved Son, with whom I am well pleased" (Mt. 3:16–17).

Do you see, beloved, how many and how great the blessings we would have lost, if the Lord had yielded to the exhortation of John and declined baptism? For before this, the heavens were shut and inaccessible to us. Before this baptism, we would have had to descend to the lower regions, instead of ascending to the heavenly. But not only was the Lord baptized; He also renewed the "old man," giving to him again the status of adoption. For straightaway, "the heavens were opened." A reconciliation of the visible with the invisible took place, the angels were filled with joy, the diseases of earth were healed, secret things were made known, those at enmity were restored to amity. For you have heard the word of the Evangelist

Matthew, who tells us that "the heavens were opened" in three wondrous ways. When Christ the Bridegroom was baptized, the bridal chamber of heaven opened its brilliant gates. The heavens opened in like manner when the Holy Spirit descended in the form of a dove. Finally, the Father's voice spread everywhere, calling for the gates of heaven to be lifted up (cf. Ps. 24:7). "[A]nd lo, a voice from heaven, saying, "This is my beloved Son, with whom I am well pleased."

The beloved generates love, and the light immaterial begets the light inaccessible. "This is my beloved Son." While on earth He is yet united to the Father's bosom, the Son was manifested in visible form, although not appearing in His fullness. He was far more than He appeared to the onlookers at the Jordan—for in appearance John, the baptizer, seems to be superior to the One baptized. For this reason, the Father sent the Holy Spirit down from heaven upon Jesus. Just as at the time of Noah the love of God toward man was signified by the dove, so also now the Spirit, descending in the form of a dove, bearing as it were the fruit of the olive branch, rested on Jesus to give testimony concerning Him. This was so that the faithfulness of the Father's voice might be made known, and so that the prophecy of a long time past might be ratified: "The voice of the LORD is upon the waters; the glory of God thunders, the LORD, upon many waters" (Ps. 29:3). And the voice of the Lord speaks from the heavens, over the waters of the Jordan: "'This is my beloved Son, with whom I am well pleased.' This is He who is called the son of Joseph, and who, according to the divine essence, is My Only-begotten. This is my beloved Son—He who is hungry and yet feeds the multitudes, who is weary and yet gives rest to the weary, who has nowhere to lay His head (Lk. 9:5) and yet carries all things in His hand, who suffers and yet heals sufferings, who is smitten and yet confers liberty on the world (Heb. 1:3), who is pierced in the side (Mt. 26:67) and yet repairs the side of Adam."

I ask you to give me now your full attention, for I wish to return to the fountain of life and to consider this fountain, which gushes with healing. The Father of Immortality sent the Immortal Son and Word into the world, in order to wash man with water and the Spirit. He, giving us a new birth to incorruption of soul and body, breathed into us the breath (spirit) of life, and endowed us with incorruptibility. If, therefore, man has acquired an imperishable inheritance by water and the Holy Spirit, he will also be found co-heir with Christ (Rom. 8:17) after the resurrection from the dead.

Therefore I preach: Come, peoples of all nations, to the immortality of Baptism. I bring good tidings of life to you who linger in the darkness of ignorance. Come into liberty from slavery, into a kingdom from tyranny, into incorruption from corruption. And how, you ask, shall we come? How? By water and the Holy Spirit. This is the water joined with the Spirit, by which paradise is watered, by which the earth is enriched, by which plants grow, by which animals multiply, and—to sum up the whole in a single phrase—by which we are born again and endowed with life. In this manner, Christ was also baptized, and the Spirit descended in the form of a dove.

This is the same Spirit that at the beginning "was moving over the face of the waters" (Gen. 1:2), by whom the world moves, through whom creation exists, and by whom all things have life. This is the Spirit who also worked mightily in the prophets (Acts 28:25) and descended upon Christ (Mt. 3:16). This is the Spirit who was given to the apostles in the form of fiery tongues (Acts 2:3). This is the Spirit whom David sought when he said, "Create in me a clean heart, O God, and put a new and right spirit within me" (Ps. 51:10). Of this Spirit, Gabriel also spoke to the Virgin: "The Holy Spirit will come upon you, and the power of the Most High will overshadow you" (Lk. 1:35). By this Spirit, Peter spoke that blessed word: "You are the Christ, the Son of the living God" (Mt. 16:16). By this Spirit, the rock of the Church was established (Mt. 16:18). This is the Spirit, the Comforter, who is sent upon Jesus (Jn. 16:26), that He might show Him to be the Son of God.

Come, then, and be born again into the adoption of God. No longer practice adultery, do not commit murder, and serve no idols. Do not be mastered by pleasure, do not allow pride to rule you, cleanse yourself of the filthiness of impurity, and put off the burden of sin. Cast off the armor of the devil and put on the breastplate of faith. As Isaiah says, "Wash yourselves; make yourselves clean; remove the evil of your doings from before my eyes; cease to do evil, learn to do good; seek justice, correct oppression; defend the fatherless, plead for the widow. Come now, let us reason together, says the LORD: though your sins are like scarlet, they shall be as white as snow; though they are red like crimson, they shall become like wool. If you are willing and obedient, you shall eat the good of the land" (Is. 1:16–19). Do you see, beloved, how the prophet spoke of the purifying power of Baptism? For he who comes in faith to the water of regeneration and renounces the devil, joining himself to Christ; he who denies the enemy and makes the confession that Christ is God; he who puts off slavery and puts on the adoption—this is he who comes up from baptism brilliant as the sun, flashing forth the beams of righteousness, and, most importantly, returns a son of God and co-heir with Christ.

To God be the glory and the power, together with His most holy, good, and life-giving Spirit, now and forever, to all the ends of the ages. Amen.

The Wedding of Cana

Another mystery of light is the first of the signs, given at Cana (cf. Jn. 2:1–12), when Christ changes water into wine and opens the hearts of the disciples to faith, thanks to the intervention of Mary, the first among believers.

—*John Paul II*, Rosarium Virginis Mariae

The First of Christ's Signs

On the third day there was a marriage at Cana in Galilee, and the mother of Jesus was there; Jesus also was invited to the marriage, with his disciples. When the wine failed, the mother of Jesus said to him, "They have no wine." And Jesus said to her, "O woman, what have you to do with me? My hour has not yet come." His mother said to the servants, "Do whatever he tells you." Now six stone jars were standing there, for the Jewish rites of purification, each holding twenty or thirty gallons. Jesus said to them, "Fill the jars with water." And they filled them up to the brim. He said to them, "Now draw some out, and take it to the steward of the feast." So they took it. When the steward of the feast tasted the water now become wine, and did not know where it came from (though the servants who had drawn the water knew), the steward of the feast called the bridegroom and said to him, "Every man serves the good wine first; and when men have drunk freely, then the poor wine; but you have kept the good wine until now." This, the first of his signs, Jesus did at Cana in Galilee, and manifested his glory; and his disciples believed in him. (Jn. 2:1–11)

This beautiful and profound story opens the second chapter of Saint John's Gospel. The first chapter of John's Gospel maps out for us, through symbolic language, who Jesus is and what He has come to do. At the very beginning of John, the Prologue says: "In the Beginning was the Word, and the Word was with God, and the Word was God. He was in the beginning with God; all things were made through him" (Jn. 1:1–3). These words with which John begins his Gospel echo back to the words that begin all of Scripture in Genesis: "In the beginning God created the heavens and the earth" (Gen. 1:1). John is calling us back to the first creation, and in doing so, he sets the stage for the telling of a new creation in Jesus. The God who created the physical world is about to usher in a new creation through His Son.

"On the Third Day"

The simple phrase "on the third day" is often overlooked in the story of Cana, but it is a crucial detail in linking this story to the Genesis creation account. Saint John makes careful mention of the order of these days for a very important reason. John 2:1 explicitly states that the wedding at Cana took place "on the third day." However, in chapter 1 of his Gospel, John records four "days" that precede this "third day" mentioned in chapter 2. If we look at each day in sequence, we will understand that the miracle at the wedding of Cana actually occurs on the *seventh* of a series of days recorded by John.

On the first day mentioned in John's Gospel (Jn. 1:19–28), John the Baptist tells his followers that he is not the Messiah, but the messenger who comes before him: "I am the voice of one crying in the wilderness, 'Make straight the way of the Lord,' as the prophet Isaiah said" (Jn. 1:23). Verse 29 introduces the second day: "The next day . . ." On this second day, John the Baptist proclaims that Jesus was revealed as the Son of God at His baptism, as the Spirit descended upon Him. Day three starts in verse 35 with "the next day again . . ." On this day, Andrew and another apostle go to stay with Jesus to see His way of life, and they become convinced that He is the Messiah sent from God (Jn. 1:39). Andrew runs to Simon Peter, his brother, and tells him, "We have found the Messiah" (Jn. 1:41). On the fourth day, "the next day," Jesus goes to Galilee (v. 43). Nathanael begins to follow Jesus with the exclamation: "Rabbi, you are the Son of God! You are the King of Israel!" (Jn. 1:49).

In each of these four days mentioned, someone makes a statement about who Jesus really is—Messiah, Rabbi, Son of God. These insights from the followers of Jesus in the Gospel of John point to both His identity and His mission. On the seventh day, Jesus is going to manifest Himself and confirm the statements of His followers.

The seventh day is found at the very beginning of the second chapter of John: "On the third day there was a marriage at Cana in Galilee" (Jn. 2:1). Saint John reveals that this is the third day *after* the fourth day mentioned in verse 43 of his first chapter. This makes it the seventh day recorded in the Gospel of John.

In the seven days of the first creation, the sun, moon, stars, earth, wind, and fire were all created *ex nihilo*, out of nothing. In this new creation, starting at the wedding feast, Jesus is taking water, something already created, to a whole new level and dimension. The first creation was a physical creation of the natural world; the new creation account given by John is a spiritual creation of the super-natural order.

The miracle at the wedding of Cana gives us insight into Jesus' plan and mission. Before this account, Jesus had not performed any miracles. No one would have known Him from Adam. When Nathanael heard about Jesus he asked, "Can anything good come out of Nazareth?" (Jn. 1:46). This miracle by Jesus at Cana highlights what He came to do—to restore the intimate relationship between God and His creation lost by Adam and Eve. The disobedience of our first parents led to the fall of creation; John, in his Gospel, highlights that the new creation starts with the obedience of a man and a woman—Jesus and Mary.

In Adam, we fell down in sin and suffered separation from God; in Jesus Christ, we begin to "fall up," back into a relationship with our Heavenly Father. He begins to re-do what Adam had undone. We "fall up" to a greater degree than we fell down. At Cana this is demonstrated by the overabundance of the water turned wine. The Church highlights this at the Easter Vigil: "O happy fault, O necessary sin of Adam, which gained for us so great a Redeemer!"[1] Jesus begins the work of redemption and restoration to the Father with His first public miracle at Cana.

---

[1] "The Easter Proclamation," International Commission on English in the Liturgy, *The Sacramentary* (New York: Catholic Book Publishing, 1985), 184.

"There Was a Marriage at Cana in Galilee"

Jesus begins His ministry with a wedding feast and ends it with the Passover feast. Is there any connection between the two? The *Catechism* tells us that the wedding of Cana "is the sign of another feast—that of the wedding of the Lamb where he gives his body and blood at the request of the Church, his Bride" (no. 2618). In Revelation, the last book of the Bible (also written by John), the great Eucharistic banquet of the Mass is described as a wedding feast: "Let us rejoice and exult and give him the glory, for the marriage of the Lamb has come, and his Bride has made herself ready" (Rev. 19:7). Jesus is the Lamb throughout the Book of Revelation; the Bride is the Church. Then the angel tells Saint John, "Write this: Blessed are those who are invited to the marriage supper of the Lamb" (Rev. 19:9). These same words are proclaimed in Mass, right before the priest and people receive Jesus in the Eucharist. Every time we go to Mass, we are participating in the Last Supper, which is the great wedding feast of Jesus and His Church. The wedding of Cana points toward this greater reality of the wedding feast of the Lamb.

If you read closely the passage of the wedding feast at Cana, you will notice that the couple's names are not mentioned. John omitted them under the inspiration of the Holy Spirit. Saint Augustine once commented that the names of the couple were withheld in order to symbolize the marriage between Christ and the Church. It is indeed no coincidence that Jesus, at the start of His ministry, chooses to manifest Himself at a wedding. Marriage is the start of a new, shared life and a new beginning. By performing His first miracle at the start of this couple's new life together,

Jesus reveals the great intimacy that God desires to have with all His people. The love between God and His people is like the love between a bridegroom and his bride.

John the Baptist saw himself as a key figure in the divine romance between Christ and the Church. In the chapter after the wedding of Cana, John says, "You yourselves bear me witness, that I said, I am not the Christ, but I have been sent before him. He who has the bride is the bridegroom; the friend of the bridegroom, who stands and hears him, rejoices greatly at the bridegroom's voice; therefore this joy of mine is now full" (Jn. 3:28–29). John sees himself as the friend of the bridegroom, Jesus. At the wedding feast, Jesus brings to light His desire for the new beginning and the new intimacy that He plans to bring to the people of God. Jesus, as the Divine Suitor, woos the hearts of His people.

"They Have No Wine"

So often we forget that Scripture describes real life. It is easy to be passive readers, failing to imagine the events as they might have been, as you would when reading a novel. Keep in mind that this Gospel story really did happen, and try to put yourself there. Imagine the scene: this was the day that the newly married couple had been anticipating with excitement for some time. And they were not alone—in a village like Cana, the whole town would have come to the wedding feast! In fact, in their tradition, a wedding was such a major event that it was celebrated for seven days. At this wedding, however, despite all the careful preparations, the unthinkable happened—the wine "failed." A wedding without wine would have been a poorly done affair in first-century Jewish culture. A feast that was supposed to be full of joy for the wedded couple would have been filled with embarrassment—they would have felt that they had not provided well for the guests. After such a disaster, the feast would have been known as "the wedding where the wine ran out." Mary, in her generosity of heart, wanted to spare the couple this disappointment.

In Scripture, we most often see Mary only in the background. Although we know that her role was essential and important, it is rarely recorded specifically. The wedding of Cana is a unique moment in the Scriptures where we get a glimpse of what Mary is all about. Saint Edith Stein says of her: "Mary at the wedding of Cana in her quiet, observing look surveys everything and discovers what is lacking. Before anything is noticed, even before the embarrassment sets in, she has procured already the remedy. She finds ways and means, she gives necessary directives, doing all quietly. She draws no attention to herself."[2] Mary wants the newly married couple to enjoy the celebration, and so she attentively looks to their needs. She has an outward focus that is selfless; she is fundamentally orientated to others. Mary desires to serve. Having already given her whole life to the service of God and others, she does what comes naturally for her: she takes the needs of the couple directly to Jesus.

Christ is described in Philippians 2:5–7: "Have this mind among yourselves, which was in Christ Jesus, who, though he was in the form of God, did not count equali-

---

[2] Saint Edith Stein, *The Collected Works of Edith Stein, Vol. 2: Woman*, 2nd ed., ed. L. Gelber and Roamaeus Lueven, trans. Freda Mary Oben (n.p.: ICS Publications, 1996), 51.

ty with God a thing to be grasped, but emptied himself, taking the form of a servant, being born in the likeness of men. And being found in human form he humbled himself and became obedient unto death, even death on a cross." This same Scripture could also describe Mary's attitude of humble service. As the Mother of God, she really did deserve to have a place of honor at the feast and to be served by others. Instead, *she* is the one who is serving, giving honor to the newly married couple. Mary's willingness to serve echoes that of her Son, "who came not to be served but to serve, and to give his life as a ransom for many" (Mk. 10:44).

Both at the wedding feast in Cana and at the foot of the Cross, John calls Mary "woman." The use of "woman" in these passages in reference to Mary is highly symbolic. At the beginning of John's Gospel, we see Mary at the wedding feast, acting as a mother to this newly married couple by bringing their need to Jesus. At the end of this Gospel, we see Jesus giving His mother to "the disciple whom he loved" (Jn. 19:26). Jesus says to John, "Behold, your mother!" (Jn. 19:27). And to Mary, He says, "Woman, behold your son!" (v. 26). Symbolically, the Apostle stands in for all of the followers of Christ; therefore, Jesus gives Mary to be our mother, too.

Mary's role at the wedding feast gives us insight into what her role as our mother will be. She will act as an intercessor, as an advocate: "At the wedding of Cana the Gospel clearly shows the power of Mary's intercession as she makes known to Jesus the needs of others: 'They have no wine'" (*RVM* 16). She brings our petitions to Jesus. Most children know that the best way to get Dad to say "yes" to something they really want is to ask Mom to intercede for them. The same is true of our heavenly Mother. Just as Mary interceded for the couple at the wedding feast, so also, as Mother of the Church, does she take our needs before the throne of her Son in heaven.

Mary's role as mother is clear from the context in this passage, as well as from the passage of the Crucifixion. There is also another context, taken straight from the Old Testament, in which we can see Mary's role. We in the twenty-first century often have a hard time seeing things from the perspective of the first-century Jews because we are completely disconnected from the way that they viewed the world. For instance, we would typically think of a queen as the wife of a king, right? That, however, is not the way that things worked in the land of Israel. For example, King Solomon had over seven hundred wives, not to mention hundreds of concubines. How could they all be queen? King Solomon, however, had only one mother, Bathsheba. Thus, the mother traditionally reigned over Israel with the king, her son. She was called *gebirah*, or "queen mother." An example of this is found in 1 Kings 2:19–21, when Bathsheba comes to King Solomon to make a petition. He bows down to her, and then has her sit at his right hand. In their culture, where one was seated denoted one's social status. To sit at King Solomon's right hand meant that Queen Bathsheba was second in authority.

The queen mother had a special role in the kingdom of Israel—advocate. She brought the needs of the people before the king. We will again use Queen Bathsheba as our example. In 1 Kings 2:13–18, Adonijah asks Bathsheba to bring a request to King Solomon. Adonijah knows to go to Bathsheba, because she, as the queen mother, has the king's ear. Bathsheba proceeds to make supplication to King Solomon in verses 19–21. Solomon says to Bathsheba, "Make your request, my mother; for I will not refuse you" (v. 20). Solomon has Bathsheba sit at his right hand, reserved for those second in command, and then tells her that he will do whatever she wants! This foreshadows the intercessory role of the Mother of Jesus, the greatest and last King of Israel. She, like her Old Testament counterparts, brings the petitions of her children before the throne of Jesus Christ in heaven.

"My Hour Has Not Yet Come"

Have you ever wondered about the strange response at Cana of Jesus to Mary, "My hour has not yet come" (Jn. 2:4)? Throughout John's Gospel, Jesus often talks about "the hour." At the end of His time on earth, Jesus again mentions "the hour." The context is the Last Supper: "Now before the feast of the Passover, when Jesus knew that his hour had come to depart out of this world to the Father, having loved his own who were in the world, he loved them to the end" (Jn. 13:1). Jesus' hour, then, is linked to His death. Before He is captured in the Garden, He prays, "Father, the hour has come; glorify thy Son that the Son may glorify thee" (Jn. 17:1). The hour that Jesus alludes to at Cana is fulfilled at His Passion and death. The way in which Jesus begins His public ministry at the wedding of Cana is a clue to how He will end it. In a sense, He begins with the end in mind. Through His first sign, Jesus foreshadows the way that He will end His mission.

"Do Whatever He Tells You"

"The first of the 'signs' worked by Jesus—the changing of the water into wine at the marriage in Cana—clearly presents Mary in the guise of a teacher, as she urges the servants to do what Jesus commands" (*RVM* 14). Mary's request, "Do whatever he tells you," is the principle for our life in Christ. Mary does not try to run the show; she does not need to be intricately involved in the miracle. She simply tells the servants to listen to Jesus, placing all the attention on her Son. This is the "luminous principle," according to John Paul II in his encyclical on the Rosary: "The role of Mary, totally grounded in that of Christ and radically subordinated to it, 'in no way obscures or diminishes the unique mediation of Christ, but rather shows its power'" (*RVM* 15).

The servants at the feast are usually the forgotten characters in this story, but they play an important role in the miracle nevertheless. Mary invites them to follow Jesus' instructions, which they do. They are attentive to Mary and ready to act on Jesus' words. Mary's entreaty, "Do whatever he tells you," is not only addressed to the servants at the feast, but it is meant for all of the servants of Christ. According to John Paul II, it is "the great maternal counsel which Mary addresses to the Church of every age" (*RVM* 21). We all have a part to play in God's plan. It may be as simple, yet as vital, as filling up the water jars so that Jesus can change them into wine.

"Six Stone Jars Were Standing There"

John tells us "six stone jars were standing there, for the Jewish rites of purification, each holding twenty or thirty gallons" (Jn. 2:6). What were these jars for purification doing at this wedding? If we read on, the passage tells us, "the Passover of the Jews was at hand" (Jn. 2:13). The wedding is taking place right before the great Jewish feast of Passover. This holy day, celebrated every year, commemorates the rescue of the Israelites from the Egyptians, who were the enemies of Israel at the time of the Exodus. When Christ begins His public ministry, He combats Israel's real enemy—Satan.

Before going to worship for a feast, the Jews would ritually wash themselves with water as an external sign of their cleansed interior hearts. Jesus uses the ritual water jugs to perform the miracle of Cana and, by doing so, identifies His mission with a real cleansing—the cleansing of sin. This cleansing will come about not by water, but by His blood on the Cross.

The Feast of the Passover is mentioned three times in John's Gospel. The first time is immediately after the wedding of Cana, where Jesus transforms the water into wine. The second time the Passover is mentioned, John 6:4, Jesus multiplies five loaves and two fish to feed over five thousand people. After the miracle of the multiplication of the loaves, He goes on to speak of Himself as the Bread of Life that came down from heaven. Jesus tells the crowd: "Truly, truly, I say to you, unless you eat the flesh of the Son of man and drink his blood, you have no life in you" (Jn. 6:53). Jesus predicts that one day He will offer His body and blood as real food and drink.

The third and final time the Passover is mentioned in John is at the time of the Last Supper (see Jn. 13:1). In Matthew's account of the Last Supper, we see where bread and wine are used. Jesus takes bread and says, "This is my body." Then Jesus takes the wine and says, "This is my blood" (Mt. 26:26–28). Here, at the Last Supper, the bread and wine find their fulfilled meanings. Jesus was preparing His listeners for the full revelation of Himself in the Eucharist.

"The Disciples Believed in Him"

Saint John's Gospel has been called "the book of signs." There are several signs and miracles that are significant in Jesus' public ministry. Scripture tells us: "This, the first of his signs, Jesus did at Cana in Galilee, and manifested his glory; and the disciples believed in him" (Jn. 2:11). By changing water into wine, Jesus manifested His glory. Pope John Paul II, in his letter on the Rosary, quotes the *Catechism*: "Everything in the life of Jesus is a sign of his Mystery" (*RVM* 24; cf. no. 515). The glory of the miracle sheds light upon who Jesus is. "And the Word became flesh and dwelt among us, full of grace and truth; we have beheld his glory, glory as of the only Son from the Father" (Jn. 1:14). The glory He manifested at Cana was that of the Son of the eternal Father.

From this point on, the disciples believed in Him. This miracle was a luminous event for them, as it shed light on the person of Jesus. John Paul II writes, "Christ changes water into wine and opens the hearts of the disciples to faith; thanks to the intervention of Mary, the first among believers" (*RVM* 21). The disciples were open to the gift of faith and received it when they open-mindedly witnessed the miracle at Cana.

* * * *

Let us pray for the fruit of discipleship to Jesus through Mary.

At Cana, because of Mary's request to Jesus, the disciples of Christ saw His first supernatural sign and began to believe in Him. We pray that, through Mary, we too may become better disciples of Jesus and that our faith may grow as we follow Him. Amen.

Points for Reflection

1. Have you ever thought of the Mass as a great wedding banquet? Is this different from the way that you normally view the Mass? Jesus, the Bridegroom, poured out His life for the Church, His Bride, even to the point of death on the Cross, and continues to give Himself in the Eucharist. If you are married, does your marriage reflect the marriage between Christ and the Church?

2. How often do you imitate Mary and look to the needs of others? Contemplate Mary's selfless service and attentiveness to the newly married couple at the wedding. Think of your state in life (married, single, religious). Think of your day-to-day life. In what practical ways can you be attentive to others?

3. Mary is the Mother of the Church. "As such, she continually brings to birth children for the mystical Body of her Son. She does so through her intercession, imploring upon them the inexhaustible outpouring of the Spirit" (*RVM* 15). Do you see Mary as your mother? Do you rely on Mary's intercession? She was concerned about the lack of wine at the wedding feast. Do you ask

her to intercede for you in the little things, in the small details of life that don't seem important?

4. "Do whatever he tells you." Mary places all the attention on Jesus. She did not try to tell the servants what to do; she directed them to Jesus. Do you ever want to run the show? Do you want your share in the lime-light, even to the point of excluding Christ? What is Jesus telling you to do in your life? Do you see that your role is just as important and vital as the servants' role in Jesus' first miracle?

5. What are those things that need to be transformed in your heart, like water into wine? Do you make yourself "good water," ready to be transformed by the Holy Spirit in the sacraments? Do you allow yourself to be filled to the brim with virtue, prayer, and good deeds, so that Christ can transform you?

6. Mary's trust in her Son was absolute and complete. Do you have trust in Jesus as Mary did? Do you believe that He can heal us and change us? Do you believe that He has a good plan for our lives? How can you trust Jesus more with the problems in your life?

7. The Holy Father tells us, "Mary lives only in Christ and for Christ!" (*RVM* 15). How can you live out more fully this whole-hearted commitment to Christ in your life and in your relationships with others?

Reflections from the Fathers

Saint John Chrysostom

"O woman, what have you to do with me? My hour has not yet come" (Jn. 2:4). This is no slight question that we ponder today. For at first, when the mother of Jesus says, "They have no wine," Christ replies, "O woman, what have you to do with me? My hour has not yet come" (Jn. 2: 3–4). Then, even though He said this, He nonetheless did as His mother had asked—an action that is worth considering. Let us then, after calling upon Him who worked the miracle, proceed to the explanation.

The words "My hour has not yet come" are not used only in this place, but also in other places in Scripture. The same evangelist, John, says, "[N]o one arrested him, because his hour had not yet come" (Jn. 8:20). And again: "So they sought to arrest him; but no one laid hands on him, because his hour had not yet come" (Jn. 7:30). And again: "Father, the hour has come; glorify thy Son" (Jn.

"Reflections from the Fathers: Saint John Chrysostom" is an adaptation of selections from Homily 22, in *Nicene and Post- Nicene Fathers*, 1st ser., vol. 14; available from www.ccel.org. Adapted from the 1888 edition, Christian Literature Publishing.

17:1). What do these words mean? What is their explanation? Christ did not say "My hour has not yet come"
because He was subject to time—the passing of seasons,
or the observance of an "hour." How could He be, since
He is the Maker of seasons, and the Creator of the times
and the ages? So to what, then, is He alluding?

Christ desires to show us that He works all things in
their proper season, and not all at once. Confusion and dis-
order would have ensued, if, instead of working all at their
proper seasons, He had mixed all together—His Birth, His
Resurrection, and His coming to Judgment. Observe that
creation did not occur all at once; man and woman were
created, but they were not created at the same time.
Mankind was condemned to death, and yet there was to be
a resurrection; but the interval between the two would be
great. The law was given, but grace was not yet given with
it; each was to be dispensed at its proper time.

Now, Christ was not subject to the time, but rather set
everything in proper order, since He is the Creator.
Therefore He said in the second chapter of John, "My
hour has not yet come." And His meaning is that He was
not as yet manifest to all, nor had He yet gathered His
whole company of disciples. Andrew followed Him, and
Philip as well, but no one else. Moreover, no one, not even
His mother or His disciples, knew Him fully; for after His
many miracles, the evangelist says, "For even his brethren
did not believe in him" (Jn. 7:5). And those at the wedding did not know Him, for, if they did, in their need they
would certainly have come to Him and begged Him for
help. Therefore Jesus said, "My hour has not yet come";
that is, "Those attending the wedding don't realize who it

is that is in their midst, nor are they even aware that the wine has run out. Let them first be aware of the situation. You should not have told me about it, My mother, for this renders the miracle suspicious. They who wanted the wine should have come and sought Me directly—not that I need this recognition, but so that they might fully assent to the miracle. For one who knows what he needs is very grateful when he obtains assistance; but one who does not realize his need will never have a plain and clear sense of the benefit."

Why then, after Jesus had said, "My hour has not yet come," and had denied her request, did He nevertheless do what His mother desired? It was done so that those who opposed Him, and thought that He was subject to the "hour," might have sufficient proof that He was not subject to any hour. If Jesus was constrained by the limits of time, how could He, before the proper "hour" had come, have done what He did? Also, He performed the miracle to honor His mother, so that He, in presence of so many, might not seem to contradict and shame her that bore Him, and also that He might not be thought to lack power, for she brought the servants to Him.

Recall that even while saying to the Canaanite woman, "It is not fair to take the children's bread and throw it to the dogs" (Mt. 15:26), Jesus nonetheless gave her "bread" because of her perseverance. Also even after saying, "I was sent only to the lost sheep of the house of Israel," He nonetheless healed the woman's daughter. From this we learn that, although we are unworthy, we often make ourselves worthy to receive God's gifts through perseverance. For this reason, His mother persevered and openly brought the servants to Him, that the request might be made by a greater number—and she told them, "Do whatever he tells you" (Jn. 2:5).

She knew that His refusal proceeded not from lack of power, but from humility, that He might not seem to hurry to the miracle without cause. Therefore, she brought the servants.

"Now six stone jars were standing there, for the Jewish rites of purification, each holding twenty or thirty gallons. Jesus said to them, 'Fill the jars with water.' And they filled them up to the brim" (Jn. 2:6–7). There is good reason that the evangelist says, "for the Jewish rites of purification." He mentions this so that none of the unbelievers could argue that there was a little wine left in the vessels, and that water was poured in and was mixed with the wine, and thus a very weak wine was made. Therefore John tells us that the vessels were "for the Jewish rites of purification," to show that those vessels were never receptacles for wine. Palestine is a country with little water, and brooks and fountains were not found everywhere. The people would always fill pots with water, so that they would have it available as a means of purification whenever they received visitors.

"And why did He not perform the miracle before they filled the vessels, which would have been even more marvelous? It is one thing to change given matter to a different quality, and quite another to create matter out of nothing." This would indeed have been more wonderful, but it would not have been so believable to those who were not actual witnesses to the miracle. Often Jesus purposely lessens the greatness of His miracles so that they may be more readily received.

"But why," one may ask, "did He Himself not miraculously produce the water that He afterwards turned into wine, instead of telling the servants to bring it?" He did it so that those who brought the water might be witnesses without any delusions. Thus, if anyone had been inclined to question the miracle, those servants could say to them, "We drew the water, we filled the vessels."

Also, in addition to what we have mentioned, by doing the miracle in this specific way Jesus counters some of the false doctrines that spring up against the Church. There are some who say that the Creator of the world is not Jesus but someone else, and that the things of this world are not Christ's works, but rather the work of some other, opposing god. To curb the madness of such unbelief, Jesus did most of His miracles on matter that He found at hand. If there had been some other, opposing god, Jesus would not have used that other's creation to show His own power. But to show that He is God—the same God who sends the rain and makes the water travel through the vine to ripen the fruit that is made into wine—He effected this change of water into wine, which happens slowly in the plant, in a moment at the wedding.

When they had filled the water pots, he said, "'Now draw some out, and take it to the steward of the feast.' So they took it. When the steward of the feast tasted the water now become wine and did not know where it came from (though the servants who had drawn the water knew), the steward of the feast called the bridegroom and said, 'Every man serves the good wine first; and when men have drunk freely, then the poor wine; but you have kept the good wine until now'" (Jn. 2:8–10).

Here again some might mock, saying, "This was an assembly of drunken men. The perception of these judges was therefore unreliable. They could not taste what was made, nor ascertain what was done. They would be unable to know whether what was made was water or wine, for they were drunk." Now this is totally ridiculous for the evangelist has removed this objection. He does not say that the guests gave their opinion on the matter, but rather that "the ruler of the feast," who was sober and had not as yet had anything to drink, gave the testimony. You are of course aware that those who are entrusted with the management of such banquets are the most sober, for it is their responsibility to conduct things with order and regularity. Therefore, the Lord called such a man of sober senses to testify to the miracle. For Jesus did not say, "Pour the wine to those that sit at table," but, "Take it to the steward of the feast."

"When the steward of the feast tasted the water now become wine, and did not know where it came from (though the servants who had drawn the water knew), the steward of the feast called the bridegroom" (Jn. 2:9–10). And why did Jesus not call upon the servants to give testimony, and so reveal the miracle? Jesus did not immediately reveal what had been done, but desired that the power of His miracles should be known over time, little by little. Suppose that it had been immediately been revealed: the servants who related it would never have been believed, but would have been thought to be mad to proclaim such testimony about one who seemed to many at that time to be a mere man. Although these servants were certain of the miracle by their own experience (for they were not likely to disbelieve their own hands), they would not have been able to convince others. And so Jesus did not reveal the miracle to all, but only to him who was best able to understand what was done, reserving the clearer knowledge of it for a future time. Thus, after the manifestation of other miracles, this one would also be credible. Later, when Jesus was about to heal the nobleman's son, the evangelist shows that the miracle at the wedding had become widely known, for it was chiefly because the nobleman knew of the miracle at the wedding feast that he called upon Jesus. John incidentally shows this when he says, "So he came again to Cana in Galilee, where he had made the water wine" (Jn. 4:46). And not just any wine, but the best.

Such are the miraculous works of Christ—they are far better and more perfect than the operations of nature. This is also seen in other instances: whenever He restored any infirm part of the body, He made it better than sound.

Not only the servants, but also the bridegroom and the ruler of the feast would testify that the wine that had been made was the best of wine. And those who drew the water would testify that Christ made it, so that, the miracle could not be ignored in the end, since He had provided so many convincing testimonies for the future. That Christ had made the water into wine, He had the servants for witnesses; that the wine that had been made was good, He had the witness of the steward of the feast and the bridegroom.

It might be expected that the bridegroom would have some reply to the steward's remark; but the evangelist, hastening to more pressing matters, has only touched upon this miracle and passed on. For what we needed to learn was that Christ made the water wine, and good wine at that; but what the bridegroom said to the steward, John did not think it necessary to add. Just so, many miracles that are at first somewhat obscure have, in the process of time, become plainer when reported more exactly by those who knew them from the beginning.

At that time, then, Jesus made of water, wine; and both then and now, He continues to transform our weak and unstable wills. For there are men who hardly differ from water, so cold, weak, and unsettled are they. But let us bring those of such disposition to the Lord, that He may change their will to the quality of wine, so that they may no longer be wishy-washy, but have body, and be the cause of gladness to themselves and others.

But who are those whose hearts are cold? They are those who give their minds to the fleeting things of this present life, and who do not turn from this world's luxury. They are those who are lovers of glory and dominion. All these things are no more than flowing waters, never stable and ever rushing violently down the steep hill. For where there is satiety, there desire cannot be; and where there is no desire, how can there be pleasure? Therefore, we find that the poor are not only healthier than the rich, and of better understanding, but also enjoy a greater degree of pleasure. Let us, when we reflect on this, flee drunkenness and luxury—not only the luxury of food and drink, but of all things that are only for this life.

Let us take in exchange the pleasure arising from spiritual things, and, as the prophet says, delight ourselves in the Lord: "Take delight in the LORD, and He will give you the desires of your heart" (Ps. 37:4). May we enjoy the good things both here and hereafter, through the grace and loving kindness of our Lord Jesus Christ, by whom and with whom, to the Father and the Holy Spirit, be glory, world without end. Amen.

The Proclamation of the Kingdom of God

Another mystery of light is the preaching by which Jesus proclaims the coming of the Kingdom of God, calls to conversion (cf. Mk. 1:15) and forgives the sins of all who draw near to him in humble trust (cf. Mk. 2:3–13; Lk. 7:47–48): the inauguration of that ministry of mercy which he continues to exercise until the end of the world, particularly through the Sacrament of Reconciliation which he has entrusted to his Church (cf. Jn. 20: 22–23).

—*John Paul II,* Rosarium Virginis Mariae

The Call to Conversion and the Forgiveness of Sins

Now after John was arrested, Jesus came into Galilee, preaching the gospel of God, and saying, "The time is fulfilled, and the kingdom of God is at hand; repent, and believe in the gospel." (Mk. 1:14–15)

"But that you may know that the Son of man has authority on earth to forgive sins"—he then said to the paralytic—"Rise, take up your bed and go home." And he rose and went home. When the crowds saw it, they were afraid, and they glorified God, who had given such authority to men. (Mt. 9:6–8)

As for what was sown on good soil, this is he who hears the word and understands it; he indeed bears fruit, and yields, in one case a hundred-fold, in another sixty, and in another thirty. (Mt. 13:1–23)

At the heart of Jesus' mission is His proclamation of the kingdom of God, best illustrated by His preaching throughout the villages of Galilee. After hearing Jesus preach, the people of Capernaum, like many in Galilee, did not want to let Him go. But He replied, "I must preach the good news of the kingdom of God to the other cities also; for I was sent for this purpose" (Lk. 4:43). Jesus identifies the Good News (the Gospel) with the kingdom of God. Indeed, He was "sent for this purpose"; that is, for the purpose of the proclamation of the kingdom. Since the kingdom is the focus of Jesus' mission, it is no wonder that Pope John Paul II has made the central Luminous mystery Jesus' proclamation of the kingdom, along with its accompanying call to conversion and the forgiveness of sins. We are, after all, taught by Jesus to "seek first his kingdom and his righteousness" (Mt. 6:33).

A problem for us in the modern world, particularly for Americans, is that the term "kingdom" sounds somewhat medieval. It strikes us as archaic; or worse, we may associate the kingdom with some kind of exclusiveness. Simply put, the idea of a kingdom to the average American is nothing more than a despot surrounded by the trappings of tradition. It is no wonder, then, that some American Scripture scholars have often replaced "kingdom of God" with "reign of God" in their contemporary translations.

The baggage that accompanies the concept of "kingdom," whether just or unjust, comes from the shortcomings and limitations of human kingdoms. But the failures of the kingdoms of men should never mar the goodness of the kingdom of God. As Jesus reminded Pilate, the kingdom of God is not "of" or "from" this world (Jn. 18:36). The answer, then, is not to simply sidestep the notion of kingdom, but rather to "supernaturalize" our understanding of it—to square our understanding of kingdom with the teaching of Jesus Christ.

"Thy Kingdom Come"

The "Our Father," given to us by Jesus as a prayer for the coming of the kingdom, illustrates that the heart of the kingdom is found in the will and love of the Father. It starts with an address to God as Father; this shows us immediately that this kingdom is about a loving Father. The prayer then moves to its first petition: that the Father's kingdom come. Parallel to asking for the kingdom to come is the seeking for His will to be done. The kingdom, therefore, is identified with the will of the Father.

Now the will of the Father is embodied not in abstract doctrines or laws, but in a person, Jesus: "My food is to do the will of him who sent me" (Jn. 4:34). "I seek not my own will but the will of him who sent me" (Jn. 5:30). And finally, that intense prayer in Gethsemane, "Abba, Father . . . not what I will, but what thou wilt" (Mk. 14:36). Jesus Himself manifests the path to the kingdom: "The kingdom will grow insofar as every person learns to turn to God in the intimacy of prayer as to a Father (cf. Lk. 11:2; Mt. 23:9) and strives to do his will (cf. Mt. 7:21)."[1] At the heart of the kingdom is our Father.

Thus the kingdom is not about power, but *persons*. Entry into this kingdom is not through golden gates; rather, one enters this kingdom by being born from on high through Baptism, because this kingdom is the family of God. The notion of the kingdom must be seen in terms

---

[1] Pope John Paul II, Encyclical on the Permanent Validity of the Church's Missionary Mandate *Redemptoris Missio* (December 7, 1990), no. 13 (hereafter cited in text as *RM*).

of the loving will of our heavenly *Abba*, which can only be understood by looking to the One who embodies this love perfectly, Jesus.

There is a mysterious identity between Jesus, the messenger of the kingdom of God, and the message. We can say that the kingdom of God is not some abstract concept or doctrine, but above all, a person, with the face and name of Jesus. As Pope John Paul II keenly observes, "The disciples recognize that the kingdom is already present in the person of Jesus and is slowly being established within humanity and the world through a mysterious connection with him" (*RM 16*). To enter into the life of the kingdom is to enter into the life of Christ. Everything Jesus taught touches on the new life that comes to each person who chooses to put the loving will of the Father into practice. The Good News is about life—a life Jesus not only taught but also lived—and we, too, are invited onto the path of life and truth. Much insight into the depths of Jesus' powerful proclamation can be gained through His parable of the sower. This story contains deep wisdom on how to make the teaching of Jesus bear fruit in our lives.

A Sower Went Out to Sow

Jesus describes His teaching about the parable of the sower as "the word of the kingdom" (Mt. 13:19). This is true in a wider sense for all Jesus' teachings, but there is a sense in which it is especially true for the parable of the sower. This parable is an overview of Jesus' proclamation of the Gospel in Galilee. In other words, the story of the sower is actually an allegorical retelling of Jesus' preaching and of the various responses His preaching elicits. The purpose of the story is to make us, the readers, reflect on how we have responded to Jesus' Word.

The sower casts his seed in four different settings, which creates four distinct responses. The sower is Jesus, and the seed is His Word about the kingdom; that is, the Gospel.

The first seed falls on the path, and the birds come and devour it. Jesus later explains the reason for the failure of the path to receive the seed: "When any one hears the word of the kingdom and does not understand it, the evil one comes and snatches away what is sown in his heart; this is what was sown along the path" (Mt. 13:19). Many times the Word of Jesus fails to take root in the depths of our hearts simply because we do not understand it. This message stands as a challenge for us: how many Catholics hear the message of Christ every Sunday, but fail to grasp its meaning? Without really having the Word explained, it can bear no fruit. Christians struggle with a broad range of issues in their everyday lives—from major issues, such as abortion, to smaller, more spiritual matters, such as exercising patience with their children—which require a deep understanding of the Gospel message. Jesus knew the first obstacle to the kingdom of God is ignorance.

The next seed falls along rocky ground, and when it springs up, having no depth of roots, it is scorched by the sun: "As for what was sown on rocky ground, this is he who hears the word and immediately receives it with joy; yet he has no root in himself, but endures for a while, and when tribulation or persecution arises on account of the word, immediately he falls away" (Mt. 13:20–21). On the surface, the kingdom of God is accepted with joy, but once that kingdom comes with a cost, it is quickly discarded. The one who has received this seed "has no root in himself." Like flowers in a vase of water, this shallow faith might last for a short while, but, having no root, it will soon fade and whither. Jesus wants us to have roots—roots that dig deep and tap into rich and constant sources of nourishment.

How can we grow in this deeply rooted faith? The just man of Psalm 1 serves as an excellent model. "He is like a tree planted by streams of water, that yields its fruit in its season, and its leaf does not wither" (Ps. 1:3). How does he do this? He avoids sinners and occasions of sin and makes the Lord his delight, constantly meditating on the Word of the Lord through prayer (Ps. 1:1–2). In other words, it is easy to be initially excited about knowing Jesus and being part of the kingdom, but growth comes only by being rooted in a long-term relationship with God.

The next seed falls among thorns, which choke the seed and keep it from growing: "As for what was sown among thorns, this is he who hears the word, but the cares of the world and the delight in riches choke the word, and it proves unfruitful" (Mt. 13:22). Many thorns threaten the "garden" of our souls in today's culture. Weeds can quickly overtake a garden, choking out its beauty; to grow something worthwhile, then, demands the untiring effort and careful tending of the gardener. Thus, if one wants a well-cultivated soul, one must work to weed out what hinders the growth of virtues and good habits in our "spiritual garden." Just as a gardener must constantly work to cultivate his garden, Jesus tells us that life in Him—that is, life in the kingdom—requires effort. We can never simply say we are Christians and let it stop at that, for the cares of the world will slowly take over the garden of our heart, and our faith will prove unfruitful.

We should be careful not to simply read this parable as if it were speaking of different kinds of people who have different responses to the Gospel. Rather, we should read this story as a warning of the different kinds of obstacles that we all must face at different times. For example, the final sowing falls upon good soil, and here, the seed brings forth an abundant harvest of grain. But the good soil is no accident—it is the place from which weeds are kept out. If we, too, wish to live an abundant life in Christ, we must free ourselves from the obstacles and cares of the world, turning our lives into good soil, rich in the knowledge of the Faith. In this way, the Gospel message can grow freely in our hearts, rooted in a deep relationship with God.

The disciples themselves were sometimes like the rocky path and hard of heart (Mk. 6:52). The kingdom was choked out of their hearts when they put their focus on worldly things, such as who would be first among them (Mk. 9:30–37). And, like the seed sown on rocky ground, they fell away from Jesus when persecution came at the arrest of Christ. However, they eventually persevered through their failures and struggles to become "good soil," practicing and preaching the Faith. We, like the disciples, are a rough garden that needs to be cleared out and carefully cultivated. No garden, not even the Garden of Eden, grows of its own accord—it must be sown and tended.

Thus, this parable is Jesus' reflection on His own preaching and its reception. The words of the kingdom contain life, like the seeds of the sower, and their fruitfulness in our lives depends on the condition of our hearts. We must care for our hearts as a gardener tends his garden. If we want the kingdom planted deep within us, we must heed the wisdom and warning contained in this story of a sower and his seed. We, too, play a part in this story. How do we receive God's Word?

"Then He Left the Crowds and Went into the House"

Like the other six parables in Matthew 13, the story of the sower is addressed to the crowds outside of Peter's house (Mt. 13:1, 34). The explanations of the parables are given only to the disciples privately, inside the house (Mt. 13:36–7). It is noteworthy that Matthew makes this distinction. The true understanding of Jesus' teaching is only found within Peter's house; Peter's house is the Church. It is only from within Peter's house, the Church, that one can see and understand the kingdom of God. Looking from within at the beautiful stained glass windows of Notre Dame in Paris, one can see their light, beauty, detail, and wonder, which are lost to those who look from without. When looking at the Church, an inside perspective is essential. John Paul II observes: "The kingdom cannot be detached either from Christ or from the Church" (*RM* 18).

Thus, the mystery of the kingdom is fully made manifest only within the Church, for the Church is the kingdom of Christ. Recall that the will of God is associated with the kingdom. The Church, then, is the normative means through which God's will for our salvation is worked out. As Vatican II observes, "To carry out the will of the Father, Christ inaugurated the Kingdom of heaven on earth and revealed to us the mystery of that kingdom. The Church, or, in other words, the kingdom of Christ already present in mystery, grows visibly through the power of God in the world."[2] Note how the Council teaches that the "kingdom of heaven" is inaugurated on "earth." This point is vital, for oftentimes when we try to picture the kingdom, we imagine it as a place high in the ephemeral heavens, where we enter through pearly gates and float along on clouds, playing harps, for eternity. But this would be to miss the beginning for the end—the present reality of the kingdom for the future.

The Kingdom of Heaven

Even though many equate the kingdom of God with heaven, this is not an accurate picture. The phrase "the kingdom of heaven," used especially in Matthew's Gospel, conveys to most of us the image of a distant kingdom in the heavens—perhaps beyond the grand cosmos. But this is not what Matthew meant. Notice that Mark and Luke often change the phrase slightly from the kingdom of heaven to the kingdom of God. Why? Matthew was a Jew, writing to a largely Jewish audience. Out of reverence for God and the holiness of His name, a Jewish tradition had developed of not speaking the name of God. *Yahweh* was only spoken in the Temple, and even then, only by the priest. And so Matthew, being a good Jew, uses the term "heaven" instead of "God," out of reverence. But Mark and Luke are writing to largely Gentile audiences

---

[2] Second Vatican Council, Dogmatic Constitution on the Church *Lumen Gentium* (November 21, 1964), no. 3 (hereafter cited in text as *LG*).

who, like us, would not understand that "heaven" stood for "God"—thus the problem. Therefore, when Jesus was talking about God's kingdom, which was being firmly planted on earth, He was not speaking about what was beyond the sky.

Unlike the Gentiles, the Jews of Jesus' day would have readily understood this. The Old Testament gives us plenty of evidence of how the Jews understood the kingdom of God as none other than the Davidic kingdom on earth. When Solomon succeeds his father David as king, we are not told that he takes the throne of David, but rather that his father declares that the Lord "has chosen Solomon my son to sit upon the throne of the kingdom of the LORD over Israel" (1 Chron. 28:5). During the enthronement celebration of Solomon, David gives a prayer of praise and thanks to God for giving his son Solomon the kingdom, and then declares that the kingdom really belongs to God. In other words, the kingdom is not David's to give, but God's: "Thine, O LORD, is the greatness, and the power, and the glory, and the victory, and the majesty; for all that is in the heavens and in the earth is thine; thine is the kingdom, O LORD, and thou art exalted as head above all" (1 Chron. 29:11). This prayer should sound familiar— David's prayer has been added to the "Our Father" during the liturgy of the Mass, as a confession that the kingdom (the Church) belongs to God!

The danger, then, is that we can come to understand that Jesus is the King, but still fail to see that the Church is the realm of His kingdom on earth. This gives us a false sense of loyalty. If we claim to love Christ and stand up for Him, but stand aloof when His kingdom is assaulted by the powers of hell or the hatred of men, we fundamentally misunderstand Jesus and His mission. We cannot dismiss the Church without dismissing Christ. Jesus came proclaiming the kingdom. How can we express loyalty to the King while we stand back and let His kingdom be assaulted? Is not the kingdom the Church, the very Bride of Christ for whom He died on the Cross? (Eph. 5). Do we really know the heart of Christ when we stand aloof, detached, or even in hostility to the Church? We do well to remember that the Church is the Body of Christ (cf. Col. 1:18; Eph. 4:12).

The Church on earth is the seed and the beginning of Christ's kingdom (*LG* 5). The Church is the kingdom of God but does not fully exhaust that kingdom. "While it slowly grows, the Church strains toward the completed Kingdom and, with all its strength, hopes and desires to be united in glory with its King" (*LG* 5). We should not think of the Church in a dualistic way—that is, that it consists of two distinct dimensions, the earthly (the Church) and the spiritual (the Mystical Body of Christ). Rather, the kingdom is one, complex reality. Just as Christ in His Incarnation is both human and divine in nature, so too is the Church. This may be a challenge to see, especially if we have taken up the habit of seeing through the lens of the world, which focuses exclusively on the human side, with all its sins and scandals. But we must see beyond the visible to the invisible. For example, as we contemplate the Eucharist, we cannot stop at the visible bread and wine, but with eyes of faith we must see the true presence of Christ—in the midst of His kingdom, the Church, here on earth.

The Call to Conversion
and the Forgiveness of Sins

One of the greatest weapons possessed by the kingdom of God on earth is the power to destroy—not soldiers—but sins. The forgiveness of sins is a sign of divine power that God has bequeathed to His Church. At the heart of Jesus' proclamation of the Good News is the call for repentance—a conversion of heart that is effected in the Sacrament of Reconciliation. When Jesus heals the paralytic, He does this as a sign of the greater healing effected by the forgiveness of sins (Mt. 9:1–7). And Jesus points out that this authority is given to Him as the Son of man *on earth*—pointing to the fact that God is now about to give the divine power to pardon sinners to men on earth.

Matthew's account reinforces this point. Jesus' forgiveness of the paralytic's sins, confirmed through physical healing, causes the crowd to glorify God, "who had given such authority to men" (Mt. 9:8). The crowds do not say to the *man*, Jesus, but to *men*, plural. Matthew wants us to understand that the authority to forgive sins, exercised by Jesus, has been given by Him to other men—namely, to the Twelve and those who are in apostolic succession to them (ordained bishops and priests). Indeed, this healing story occurs in a section of Matthew (chapters 8–9) that focuses on Jesus' authority, which prepares the reader for the next section (chapter 10), where Jesus gives the Twelve a share in His authority. The point is clear: Jesus' power to forgive has been passed on to the Twelve, who constitute the priestly leadership of His kingdom.

This point is furthered strengthened when, after Peter confesses faith in Jesus, the Lord declares, "[Y]ou are Peter, and on this rock I will build my church." Immediately following this declaration, Jesus gives Peter the "keys of the kingdom of heaven" (Mt. 16:18–19). Jesus parallels the building of the Church on Peter with the act of giving him the keys of the kingdom. Again, the identity of the Church and the kingdom are intertwined. The power of the keys is to bind and loose; this imagery concerns, among other things, the forgiveness of sins. This power to forgive sins is subsequently given to all of the twelve apostles (Mt. 18:18).

How can men, albeit ordained, wield such divine power? Can we really go to a priest and have our sins forgiven? The answer is most clearly found in Jesus' encounter with the Twelve in the upper room after His Resurrection. The Twelve are hiding in the upper room when Jesus comes and is recognized by the scars from the Crucifixion, the wounds that atone for our sins. Jesus then commissions them for a priestly mission: "'As the Father has sent me, even so I send you.' And when he had said this, he breathed on them, and said to them, 'Receive the Holy Spirit. If you forgive the sins of any, they are forgiven; if you retain the sins of any, they are retained" (Jn. 20:21–23). These men can forgive sins because they have been ordained with the power of the Holy Spirit. Jesus equips these leaders of His kingdom and sends them out with the purpose and power to forgive sins.

Jesus, the embodiment of the Kingdom, inaugurates the kingdom of God on earth as He fulfills and manifests the Father's loving will. This kingdom, then, is not about castles and courtyards, but about the love of God. And as ambassadors of that love, as Saint Paul says, His priestly ministers appeal to us to be reconciled to our heavenly Father by the sacrament of God's mercy and forgiveness, Reconciliation (2 Cor. 5:18–20). By confessing our sins to the priest, we encounter one of the many ways the Church is the kingdom of God on earth. The good news that this kingdom is open to all, despite our sins, should be a focal point of our meditation on Jesus' proclamation of the Gospel. Certainly the call to conversion and the kingdom is a luminous mystery that sheds light on the darkness of our discouragement and sins, by bringing us into the light of hope and joy, as we see the heavenly light that shines through the work of God in the Church—Heaven's kingdom on earth.

* * * *

Let us pray for the fruit of a deeper conversion.

We pray that we may come to a deeper metanoia, or conversion of the heart, and that with this deeper conversion we may share the joy of being liberated from the bondage to sin and of knowing Jesus Christ with others by proclaiming the Good News in word and deed. Amen.

Points for Reflection

1. What does it mean to seek first God's kingdom and His righteousness? Are you seeking after God's kingdom in your own life?

2. What does it mean to be a son or daughter of the King? What kind of dignity does this kingdom bestow upon us? Do you think of God the Creator, the King of heaven and earth, as a loving Father? Why or why not?

3. Do you see the will of the Father as an abstract will, or as one that is for your own good, embodied by the Person of Jesus? How have you responded to Jesus' word, to the proclamation of the kingdom?

4. How is the kingdom of God different from the kingdoms of this world? Is it hard for you to associate Jesus with a kingdom?

5. In the parable of the sower, the seed first falls on the path, and the birds come and eat it up. Do you find yourself hearing the Word, but not understanding? Do you make time to learn more about your faith in order to remedy this problem? What specifically can you do in order to learn and understand more about the kingdom of God and your relationship with Jesus?

6. Are you like the rocky soil? Can you remember a time when you were really excited about your faith, but let it fall by the wayside when things got difficult? Are you afraid to suffer for your relationship with Christ? Is it hard for you to follow through with your commitment to pray? Pray that God will give you the grace of perseverance and steadfastness.

7. What are the "thorns" in your life? Are they the cares of the world? Think about those things that choke out the good seed in your life: evil thoughts about others, selfishness, materialism, etc. It's time to do some weeding! How can you pull out those nasty thorns and weeds that threaten to kill your relationship with God?

8. How can you be the good soil in which the seed thrives? How can you learn from the lessons of the path, the rocky soil, and the thorns, in order to cultivate a garden in your soul that is rich in soil, where abundant fruit will grow?

9. Like the paralytic in Matthew, how has God healed and restored you? In what areas of your life do you still need healing?

10. When you go to the Sacrament of Reconciliation, do you really know that you are healed? Do you make this sacrament a priority in your life? Make a resolution to meet Christ in the Sacrament of Reconciliation more often.

Origen

After speaking to the multitudes, Jesus, along with His disciples, returned to His house. His disciples asked Him: "Explain to us the parable of the weeds in the field" (Mt. 13:36).

Jesus certainly loves all men, as is attested in Scripture by the fact that He regularly speaks to the crowds. But it is important to note that when Jesus sends the crowds away, He goes to His home, accompanied by His disciples. Recall how John pointed out Jesus to two of his followers. When they followed Christ and asked where He was staying, Jesus then invited them to "come and see." According to Scripture, Andrew, the brother of Simon Peter, was one of those first disciples who came to His home (Jn. 1:35–41).

If we want to experience that closeness with Jesus—to hear Him speak to us in His own house—let us also become His friends. Then, as His disciples, we too can ask

"Reflections from the Fathers: Origen" is an adaptation of selections from "Commentary on the Gospel of Matthew," bk. 10, sect. 1–15; available from www.newadvent.org.

Him to explain to us the parable of the weeds in the field, or ask Him any question. The words of the Gospel seem deceptively simple. Actually, they contain great depth of wisdom, which becomes understandable only by God's grace, to those who seek as disciples.

The Explanation of the Parable

And Jesus answered, "He who sows the good seed is the Son of man" (Mt. 13:37). The good seed is the good things of the kingdom sown in the human soul by God, the Word who was in the beginning with God (cf. Jn. 1: 2). It is the devil who sows the weeds in the souls of men who are sleeping instead of following the command of Christ: "Watch and pray that you may not enter into temptation" (Mt. 26:41).

The Son of man also sows the good seed in the field that is the entire world, and likewise the devil sows the weeds throughout the world. At the end of time, the close of the age (Mt. 13:42), there will be a harvest. The angels of God are appointed to this task. They will gather all that is evil and a stumbling block to men and throw it into the fiery furnace. Then those who have allowed the seeds of evil to grow in their souls, because they had been sleeping, will recognize their true situation. Then "men will wail and gnash their teeth" (Mt. 13:42). Above all, "the righteous will shine like the sun in the kingdom of their Father" (Mt. 13:43). Jesus then adds, "He who has ears, let him hear" (Mt. 13:43). Not only does the parable require explanation, but even the explanation cannot be understood except by the disciples who listen to Christ.

The Parable of the Treasure Hidden in a Field

"The kingdom of heaven is like a treasure hidden in a field, which a man found and covered up" (Mt. 13:44). In the previous parables, Jesus spoke to the crowd. It appears that this parable and the two that follow were spoken only to His disciples.

To understand this parable about the kingdom of heaven, we must consider the "field," the "treasure," and what the man "sells" to obtain the field. To me, it seems that the field is the Scripture of the Old Testament, which contains history, the Law, the prophets, and other thoughts that make up the entirety of the Scripture. The treasure is that which lies, as it were, under the words of the Old Testament: Christ, or the kingdom of heaven (which is Christ Himself). So Paul writes: "Christ, in whom are hid all the treasures of wisdom and knowledge" (Col. 2:3).

At this point, you may ask whether the kingdom of heaven is compared only to the treasure, or to the field and the treasure it contains. The individual who comes to the field searches the Scripture and therein finds Christ. So it is true to say that the hidden treasure of wisdom is found in Christ and in the Scripture. The person who gives up all to follow Jesus is the one who purchases the field and its treasure, Christ.

The Parable of the Pearl of Great Price

"Again, the kingdom of heaven is like a merchant in search of fine pearls" (Mt. 13: 45). When you think of the pearl merchant, recall the Scripture: "Seek and you will find . . . for every one who seeks finds" (Mt. 7:7–8).

The merchant seeks pearls and, in the process, finds the one Pearl. As Paul states, he "count[s] everything as loss because of the surpassing worth of knowing Jesus Christ" (Phil 3:8). "Everything" is the other good pearls, which pale in comparison to the very precious Pearl.

Precious is a lamp to men who are in darkness, and they need that lamp until the sunrise. Precious also is the glory in the face of Moses and the prophets, for they introduce and help us to see the glory of Christ, to whom the Father bears witness: "This is my beloved Son, with whom I am well pleased" (Mt. 3:17). Scripture tells us that "what once had splendor has come to have no splendor at all, because of the splendor that surpasses it" (2 Cor. 3:10). The glory we see now will pale in the light of that glory which is coming. And the knowledge we now possess will be as nothing when the perfect arrives.

Knowledge of the Law and the Prophets provides a foundation to faith; these certainly are "good pearls." But they are nothing in comparison to "the surpassing worth of knowing Christ" (Phil. 3:8). Scripture tells us: "For everything there is a season, and a time for every matter under heaven" (Eccles. 3:1). There is also a time to gather those goodly pearls that are found in the Scriptures of the Old Testament. They provide the elementary schooling that will lead to a deeper understanding of the meaning in the words and deeds of Christ.

*****

The Householder and His Treasury
"And [Jesus] said to them, 'Therefore every scribe who has been trained for the kingdom of heaven is like a house-

holder who brings out of his treasure what is new and what is old'" (Mt. 13:52).

He who is truly a householder is both rich and free—rich, because he is a scribe who has learned every word of the Old Testament and of the teaching of Christ. As a disciple, his riches are stored in heaven, "where neither moth nor rust consume and where thieves do not break in and steal" (Mt. 6: 20). His heart is in heaven, "for where your treasure is, there will your heart be also" (Mt. 6:21). Because of this, the true householder, the true disciple of Christ, can say, "Though a host encamp against me, my heart shall not fear" (Ps. 27:3). Robbers cannot break into a treasure that is stored in heaven. That treasure is Christ, who "raised us up with him, and made us sit with him in the heavenly places" (Eph. 2:6), and "our commonwealth is in heaven" (Phil. 3:20).

We must gather all these things into our hearts—that which is "old and new"—by attending "to the public reading of scripture, to preaching, to teaching" (1 Tim. 4:13), and by meditating "day and night" on the Law of the Lord (cf. Ps. 1:2). We find treasure not only in the Gospels, in the letters of the apostles and in Revelation, but also in the old things—in the Law, which is "a shadow of the good things to come" (Heb. 10:1), and in the Prophets.

We are to read, know, and remember the words both of the New and the Old Testament. Together they establish and confirm every word of God. Resist anyone who tries to cut off the New from the Old; recognize that there is treasure in *both*.

Jesus Himself is a householder, who from His treasury brings forth the new, which He renews in the "inner nature" (2 Cor. 4:16) of the righteous, and also brings forth the old things, "carved in letters on stone" (2 Cor. 3:7). In this way, Christ enriches His disciples, conforming them to the kingdom of heaven and making them like Himself. Christ sets His tabernacle in us, fulfilling the promise that He made: "I will live in them and move among them" (2 Cor. 6:16; cf. Lev. 26:12).

The Transfiguration

The mystery of light par excellence *is the transfiguration, traditionally believed to have taken place on Mount Tabor. The glory of the Godhead shines forth from the face of Christ as the Father commands the astonished Apostles to "listen to him" (cf. Luke 9:35 and parallels) and to prepare to experience with him the agony of the Passion, so as to come with him to the joy of the Resurrection and a life transfigured by the Holy Spirit*

—*John Paul II*, Rosarium Virginis Mariae

A Glimpse of Christ's Glory

Now about eight days after these sayings he took with him Peter and John and James, and went up on the mountain to pray. And as he was praying, the appearance of his countenance was altered, and his raiment became dazzling white. And behold, two men talked with him, Moses and Elijah, who appeared in glory and spoke of his departure, which he was to accomplish at Jerusalem. Now Peter and those who were with him were heavy with sleep but kept awake, and they saw his glory and the two men who stood with him. And as the men were parting from him, Peter said to Jesus, "Master, it is well that we are here; let us make three booths, one for you and one for Moses and one for Elijah"—not knowing what he said. As he said this, a cloud came and overshadowed them; and they were afraid as they entered the cloud. And a voice came out of the cloud, saying, "This is my Son, my Chosen; listen to him!" And when the voice had spoken, Jesus was found alone. And they kept silence and told no one in those days anything of what they had seen. (Lk. 9:28–36)[1]

---

[1] See also Mt. 17:1–9; Mk. 9:2–10; 2 Pet. 1:16–19.

Jesus had impeccable timing. His Incarnation happened, as Paul tells us, "in the fullness of time" (Gal. 4:4). During the course of His three-year ministry, many things happened only at the time that Jesus intended them. For example, while Jesus healed many during His ministry, He purposely only initiated healing on the Sabbath. And even though there were times when the authorities and people attempted to seize Him, He simply passed through the midst of them until His hour had arrived. The Transfiguration is another example of Jesus' timing certain events of His ministry. Jesus' timing of the Transfiguration not only serves to aid the disciples in understanding the truth of His self-revelation, but will also prove to be an irreplaceable source of hope for His disciples, both during the Passion and throughout their own ministries spreading the Good News.

"Now about Eight Days after These Sayings"

Just before the Transfiguration, in the same chapter of the Gospel, Luke 9, Peter confesses that Jesus is the Messiah, the "Christ of God" (Lk. 9:20). But as soon as the disciples, in the words of Peter's confession, recognize Jesus as "the Christ," Jesus quickly redefines their understanding of what it means to be the Messiah. The Christ, the Messiah, was the long-awaited King, whom many expected to victoriously liberate Israel from the Romans. The coming of this King would usher in a new Davidic kingdom of freedom for God's people. Jesus, however, reveals to His disciples that the way of the Messiah is not the way of political power and might, but rather the way of humility, suffering, and death. Jesus then goes on to say some scandalous things about what it would mean to be a follower of the Messiah: "If any man would come after me, let him deny himself and take up his cross daily and follow me" (Lk. 9:23).

To "take up one's cross" could only mean one thing in first-century Israel: Roman execution. The Roman method of execution was crucifixion, an ordeal that forced the accused to carry the crossbeam along a main road or thoroughfare, where all could witness what happens to those who rebel against Rome. To "take up one's cross" was a disquieting thought, to say the least. A modern equivalent would be telling someone to take a seat in an electric chair. There is only one interpretation of such an order— execution. This certainly would have come as a surprise to Jesus' disciples who, like other first-century Jews, were expecting victory over the Romans, not death at their hands. Peter had just proclaimed Jesus as the Christ; and Jesus, in turn, foretells His imminent death and warns His followers that they, too, will carry their crosses. This is not what they had expected! The disciples probably would have been in shock, trying to understand all that Jesus was telling them. It is these "sayings" that would have been running through the thoughts of the apostles for the eight days leading up to the Transfiguration, when Jesus allows Peter, John, and James to witness His glory on Mount Tabor.

"And as He Was Praying, the Appearance of His Countenance Was Altered"

For eight days Jesus' disciples have wondered about His self-revelation that He is going to die. In fact, Jesus is on the way to Jerusalem to do just that. Once the declaration is made that Jesus is the Christ, the new King of the Jews, it will only be a week until He is crucified in Jerusalem. The disciples are having a hard time comprehending the predictions of His death. Furthermore, their faith will be tested at the Crucifixion, and only one disciple will remain at Jesus' side at the Cross. At the Last Supper, Jesus tells Peter, "Satan demanded to have you, that he might sift you like wheat" (Lk. 22:31).

In view of the imminent trial ahead, Jesus shows His three closest disciples His glory on Mount Tabor. Jesus takes Peter, James, and John up to Mount Tabor to pray. At the top of the mountain, as they are praying, all heaven breaks loose. It starts when Jesus' face begins to glow with glory. Not only His face, but "his raiment became dazzling white" as well (Lk. 9:29). Then Moses and Elijah appear, and the three stunned disciples behold Jesus speaking with the giver of the Old Law and the great prophet. As if that is not amazing enough, a cloud envelops the disciples and Jesus, and a voice speaks from it. The Transfiguration shows the disciples that there is more to Jesus than they had previously thought. Jesus is not simply human; He is also divine. The disciples will see His death, but this glimpse of His glory is to give them hope, which will sustain them until they witness the glory of the Resurrection.

Jesus' Transfiguration in glory is not simply a manifestation of His divinity; it is also a revelation of His perfected and glorified humanity. Jesus is the fullness of what God created all of mankind to be. He reveals the Father's desire to transform humanity into the likeness of divine glory. The Transfiguration not only gives us a glimpse of Jesus' divinity, but also shows us His true humanity—a humanity that reflects the image and likeness of God in glory.

"Two Men Talked with Him, Moses and Elijah"

It is not a random assortment of Old Testament characters that assemble with Jesus on Mount Tabor. There is something very important about the presence of Moses and Elijah that sheds light upon Jesus and His mission.

The presence of Moses is especially important, considering all that happens upon Mount Tabor. The elements of Jesus' Transfiguration—a cloud, a mountain, a voice, a transformation, a feeling of fear—may seem very familiar to one who knows the Old Testament. A similar thing happened to Moses as he received the Torah (the Law) on Mount Sinai (Ex. 24:9–18, 34:29–30). Let's look at a few similarities. Moses climbs up Mount Sinai, taking with him a group of elders (three of whom are specifically named), and they behold God. Moses then goes further up Mount Sinai, where he enters a cloud covering the mountain, from which a voice calls out. There, Moses beholds the glory of the Lord (Ex. 24:15–16). Shortly after this, Moses is again on Mount Sinai (Ex. 34:29–30), and again he talks to God. When he comes down the mountain, his face is shining, and the Israelites are afraid. These same elements are found in the Transfiguration.

Why are these events repeated on Mount Tabor? Why does Jesus choose to reveal His glory in a way that would remind those present of Moses and Sinai? Jesus is showing that He is the new and greater Moses. Moses had told the Israelites, "The LORD your God will raise up for you a prophet like me from among you, from your brethren—him you shall heed" (Deut. 18:15). Now that Prophet is here. On Mount Sinai, Moses' face was transfigured with the glory of God. On Mount Tabor, Jesus' face also shines with glory, but even more than Moses', Jesus' appearance becomes "dazzling white" (Lk. 9:29). Jesus outshines Moses by radiating the glory God Himself.

On Sinai, Moses was given the Torah, the Law. On the mount of Transfiguration, a new Sinai, a new Torah is revealed. The new Torah is not the word of God written on stone tablets, but the Word made flesh. Just as a voice spoke to Moses from the cloud on Mount Sinai, a voice speaks from the cloud on Mount Tabor. The disciples, just like the Israelites of old, are afraid. The voice says: "This is my Son, my Chosen; listen to him!" (Lk. 9:35). The voice of God reveals to us that the New Law is a Person, His Son. Jesus takes the place of the Torah. It is not that the Torah is to be abolished, but that from this time forward, following the Law will not only mean heeding the Ten Commandments; it will mean imitating the life and example of Jesus Christ, our Lord.

Elijah was one of the greatest prophets of the Old Testament. Whenever Israel, and in particular Israel's kings, turned away from the Lord to follow false gods and false ways, He sent prophets to call them back. Elijah's prayer to the Lord before the wicked King Ahab and the people of Israel was "Answer me, O LORD, answer me, that his people may know that thou, O LORD, art God, and that thou hast turned their hearts back" (1 Kings 18:37). Similarly, Jesus, who is Priest, Prophet, and King, began His ministry saying, "The time is fulfilled, and the kingdom of God is at hand; repent, and believe in the gospel" (Mk. 1:15). Jesus, like the prophets of old, calls the people of Israel to repent and to turn their hearts back to God. His preaching is first and foremost a preaching of repentance and forgiveness. The Good News preached by Christ is to have the effect seen in the woman who anointed Jesus' feet: she repented, was forgiven much, and then loved much. Her heart was turned back and united to her Lord (cf. Lk. 7:36–50).

Mark records that Jesus opened His preaching with the words "The time is fulfilled" (Mk. 1:14). In the Book of Malachi, the last prophetic writing of the Old Testament, Malachi speaks about the day of the Lord that was to come. In this discourse, the Lord exhorts the people to "remember the law of my servant Moses" (Mal. 4:4) and tells them: "I will send you Elijah the prophet before the great and terrible day of the LORD comes" (Mal. 4:5). Jesus Christ, the new Moses, has come. John the Baptist, who Jesus tells us is the new Elijah, has come. Now, here on Mount Tabor, appear these two towering figures of the Old Testament, Moses and Elijah—who, according to Malachi, mark "the day of the Lord." The time of waiting is now fulfilled. The day and the hour are now near.

Like Moses, Elijah also encountered God in a special way at Mount Sinai. Elijah, dejected by the lack of faith and holiness of the people of Israel, returned to the great mount of the Lord in search of renewal. Like Moses, Elijah longed to see the glory of the Lord—a glory that was not always reflected in God's people. Just as Moses fasted forty days and nights, Elijah also made a sacred fast before approaching the mountain of God. (The only other person known to make this forty-day fast was Jesus, who, immediately after His baptism in the Jordan, set out into the wilderness to fast and pray.) When Elijah reached the mountain, he prayed and waited for God to reveal Himself. Is it not after we experience disappointment and discouragement that we, too, long to see God's face?

Elijah's pursuit was patient and persevering. After the forty days, there was a strong and mighty wind, but God was not in the wind. Then there was an earthquake, but God was not in the earthquake. Then there was fire, but God was not in the fire. Finally, there was a still, small voice, and God *was* in the still, small voice. Having heard the voice of God speak to his heart, Elijah covered his face (1 Kings 19).

Both Moses and Elijah encountered the one, true God upon the mount—but neither of them will see and understand this God fully until the revelation of Jesus upon Mount of Tabor at the Transfiguration.

"And They Spoke of His Departure"

What did Jesus discuss with Moses, the giver of the Torah, and with Elijah, the great prophet? Luke is the only evangelist who discloses the content of their conversation. They "spoke of his *departure* [literally *exodus* in Greek], which he was to accomplish at Jerusalem" (Lk. 9:31). What did Jesus accomplish in Jerusalem? He accomplished our redemption and the forgiveness of our sins. This is the new and greater "exodus" that Jesus speaks of with Moses and Elijah.

The first Exodus freed the Israelite people from slavery under Pharaoh, and brought them out of Egypt and into the Promised Land. In the New Exodus, Jesus does not bring political freedom from the Romans, as the first-century Jews expected. Instead, He brings freedom from a much greater enemy—Satan. He frees us from a much greater slavery, that of sin and death. Isaiah 52 prophesies a new exodus in which God will deliver His people. The need is clearly presented in this passage: "[L]oose the bonds from your neck, O captive daughter of Zion" (Is. 52:2). The passage goes on to describe how God will save His people: "[F]or the Lord has comforted his people, he has redeemed Jerusalem. . . . [A]nd all the ends of the earth shall see the salvation of our God" (Is. 52:9–10). The New Exodus frees our captive hearts, turning them back to the heart of God. In the first Exodus, there was a transfer of citizenship from Egypt to Israel. On the Cross, Jesus transfers our citizenship from the land of death to the land of everlasting life.

The next chapter of Isaiah is the famous "song of the suffering servant," which describes the coming Messiah (see Is. 53). The imagery of exodus—of bonds, captivity, and redemption—gives way to a startling picture of the one through whom redemption is to come. The New Exodus will not come with a victorious military battle, as many had expected; the New Exodus is to come through the suffering of the Lord's servant, who is "wounded for our transgressions," "bruised for our iniquities," made "an offering for sin," and who pours "out his soul to death" (Is. 53). The New Exodus, which Jesus will accomplish in Jerusalem, will come only at the price of His own blood.

Here, at Mount Tabor, Jesus is indeed speaking of the longed-for exodus, foretold by the prophets, for which all of Israel was eagerly waiting; but most, including the disciples, will not recognize when it is happening. Once Jesus' conversation with Moses and Elijah had finished and the glorious cloud had disappeared, Luke tells us that

Jesus "set his face to go to Jerusalem" (Lk. 9:51). The suffering Servant of the Lord was heading to accomplish His Exodus, and our redemption.

"Master, It Is Well That We Are Here"

Saint John Vianney once observed an old peasant man who often sat in the back row of his church, praying for many long hours. Saint John was intrigued by this man's devotion. One day he approached the man and asked what he did at the church for so many hours. The peasant simply replied, "I look at Him, and He looks at me." This was his prayer before the tabernacle: a gaze upon the face of Christ.

Peter says that it is *good* to be with Jesus on Mount Tabor (Lk. 9:33). There, the apostles received the gift of contemplating Jesus glorified. "For a moment," the *Catechism* says, "Jesus discloses his divine glory" on Tabor (no. 555). That is why Peter said that it was "good" to be there: the apostles were able to look upon the face of Jesus in His glory. "Contemplation is the gaze of faith, fixed on Jesus" (*Catechism,* no. 2715, emphasis omitted). It is communion with God—this is what the Christian life is all about. Peter, James, and John experienced this gaze of faith at the Transfiguration. The Church, in calling us to contemplate the mystery of light reflected on Jesus' face during the Transfiguration, is inviting us to contemplate the light reflected on the loving face of God. The Apostle Paul's words to the Corinthians are particularly relevant for our meditation on this mystery: "And we all, with unveiled face, beholding the glory of the Lord, are being changed into his likeness from one degree of glory to another" (2 Cor. 3:18).

How often did Peter, James, and John, when they were faced with trials, recall that vision of Jesus glorified? Peter recalls the events of Mount Tabor when he writes his second letter to the faithful. He says, "[W]e were eye witnesses of his majesty. For when he received honor and glory from God the Father and the voice was borne to him by the Majestic Glory, "This is my beloved Son, with whom I am well pleased," we heard this voice borne from heaven, for we were with him on the holy mountain" (2 Pet. 1:16–18). Perhaps this recollection of Jesus' splendor is what strengthened Peter and James as they were awaiting martyrdom. Or maybe the remembrance of Jesus glorified was what helped John get through many lonely years of exile. The glorification of the humanity of Christ gave them a momentary glimpse of what God had in store for them after their own death: resurrection from the dead and the glorification of their own humanity. As Saint Paul writes: "So we do not lose heart. Though our outer nature is wasting away, our inner nature is being renewed every day. For this slight momentary affliction is preparing for us an eternal weight of glory beyond all comparison" (2 Cor. 4:16–17). God has gifted us with imagination so as to be moved, just as the apostles were, through the contemplation of Jesus' face transfigured by loving glory.

"Let Us Make Three Booths"

Peter makes a strange statement during this glorious event on Mount Tabor. He says to Jesus, "[L]et us make three booths, one for you and one for Moses and one for Elijah" (Lk. 9:33). Luke gives us a clue to Peter's thoughts when he mentions that this event took place on the eighth day (Lk. 9:28). In the Jewish liturgical calendar, there is only one feast that lasts eight days: the Feast of Tabernacles (or Booths) (see Lev. 23:36).

The Feast of the Tabernacles commemorates the Exodus and, in particular, the giving of the Law upon Mount Sinai. On the eighth day of the feast, booths (or tents) are set up in remembrance of the time of the Exodus, when the ancestors of the Israelites were wandering in the desert without a home. It is possible that Jesus and His three disciples went up the mountain on that day to pray because it was the solemn high day of the Feast of Tabernacles. What better place to remember Sinai than on a mountain? Thus, Peter's comment would have been in keeping with the traditional observance of this feast.

"Listen to Him!"

Jesus embodies the Torah. The best way to know and understand the will of the Father is to look at and listen to His Son. The command, "[L]isten to him" (Lk. 9:35), echoes a poignant prophecy of Moses. As mentioned above, in Deuteronomy 18:15–18, Moses prophesies that one greater than he will come and give a new covenant and a new law. Moses concludes the prophecy with the injunction that Israel listen to the prophet: "[H]im you shall heed" (Deut. 18:15–18). In Hebrew, the word for "listen" means "to obey." The command issued by God to Israel in the time of Moses and the command given on Mount Tabor to the apostles is the same: listen and obey Him!

The story of Israel, from the time of Moses, is a trajectory of disobedience and sin. For instance, while Moses was on Mount Sinai receiving God's Law, the people of Israel were worshipping a golden calf and engaging in immoral behavior! After all God's saving works—the miracles by which He brought them out of Egypt, the parting of the Red Sea, the provision of manna and quail in the desert—they still turned away from Him. This pattern of disobedience continued throughout the entire Old Testament.

We can look at the Israelites and be tempted to say, "Why don't they get it?" We can think of the sinfulness of Israel and exclaim: "I would never have done *that*!" Yet we have to come to see that the story of Israel is *our* story. God has done miracles in our lives. He has saved us from sin and death. In Baptism, He has given us the Holy Spirit to dwell in our hearts. Every time we go to Mass, we witness the miracle of the Eucharist. Yet we often disobey, just like the Israelites. We have to pray for ears that will "listen to him" and for a heart that will heed Him. James 1:22 says: "[B]e doers of the word and not hearers only." God want us to listen not only with our ears, but also with our hearts.

Once again, we are reminded of Mary's words at Cana, "[D]o whatever he tells you." At both the second and fourth mysteries of light, Mary and God the Father, respectively, beckon us to listen to Jesus. Between these two mysteries is the mystery of Jesus' proclamation of the Gospel and call for repentance. The message is clear: the path to life and freedom, the way to change our ordinary water into the wine of divine life is to listen to Jesus and to contemplate the glory of who we are called to be in the face of Jesus. Listening to Jesus is the way to have our hearts and minds unveiled, so that we, like Peter, John, and James, can see the glory of God through meditating on the fourth mystery of light.

* * * *

*Let us pray for the fruit of belief in
the divinity of Jesus Christ.*

Jesus' divinity is often denied in modernity. We pray that the glory of God, reflected on Jesus' face, might lead us to deeper faith in the mystery of Jesus' Incarnation, that He is fully man and fully God. May the fruit of this mystery strengthen our faith and hope as we contemplate the glory of Jesus. Amen.

Points for Reflection

1. Have you ever thought about what it really means to carry your cross? Do you find yourself thanking God for the good gifts that He gives you, but rejecting and complaining about the crosses that He has placed in your life? Saint Teresa of Avila tells us, "[T]he measure of our courage in carrying the cross is the measure of our love."[2] Right now, how strong is your love and courage as you bear the crosses Christ has given you? Pray to be strengthened in your commitment to carry your cross after Christ.

2. Saint Irenaeus tells us, "The glory of God is man fully alive, and the life of man is the vision of God."[3] All of

---

[2] Saint Teresa of Avila, *The Way of Perfection*, chap. 32.
[3] Saint Irenaeus, *Against Heresies*, bk. 4, chap. 20, no. 7.

us desire to be happy, to be "fully alive." Do you consider yourself one who is "fully alive"? How can the glory of God, revealed on Mount Tabor, help you to become "fully alive"?

3. Do you find yourself strictly living a religion of the Ten Commandments? Is your faith comprised only of "dos" and "don'ts"? If so, pray that you can see God as a Person, not just a Giver of precepts. Our way is not written on stone, but on the heart and face of Jesus. Do you tend to identify more with the Old Law in your walk with God than with the glory of the New Law revealed on Tabor?

4. "The Gospel scene of Christ's Transfiguration, in which the three Apostles Peter, James, and John appear entranced by the beauty of the Redeemer, can be seen as an icon of Christian contemplation" (*RVM* 9). Have you experienced true contemplation, which is gazing on the face of Christ?

5. John Paul II says that the Transfiguration is "a foretaste of the contemplation yet to come" (*RVM* 34). Do you prepare for heaven by contemplating Christ's face every day in prayer? Do you make time for prayer as you would for your spouse, children, friends, family, etc.? Do you think of prayer as a high priority, or is it last on your "to-do" list? What are some practical ways that you can incorporate prayer into your daily schedule? (Be creative.)

6. The Feast of Tabernacles, on which the Transfiguration took place, was an important event celebrated every year. Do you celebrate the feasts of the Church with the same energy and faithfulness? How can you better prepare for and enjoy the feasts of the Church, so that you can celebrate the great acts of God in salvation history?

7. Do you ever feel like the Israelites, hearing the Law of God but unable to do it? Do you have a hard time imitating Jesus, the new Law of God? Pray for the grace of a docile heart like Mary, so that we can hear the words of Christ and see His example, and enact these things in our lives.

8. Jesus, through His death, destroyed death for all of us. We are now citizens of heaven. Do you live as one who has dual citizenship, in heaven and on earth? What are some ways that you are living only for earth? How can you live your life more like a citizen of heaven? There is so much in this world that tugs at our hearts and distracts us. Is your heart free to love God completely?

Pope St. Leo the Great

Jesus took Peter and James and his brother John and, ascending a very high mountain, showed them the brightness of His glory. For although they had recognized the majesty of God within Jesus, they had not yet seen the power of His body, wherein His Deity was contained. And therefore, rightly and significantly, Jesus had promised that some of the disciples should not taste death until they saw "the Son of man coming in his kingdom" (Mt. 16:28). He wished to make evident to these three men this kingly brilliance, which belonged to the nature of His assumed Manhood. Since the unspeakable and unapproachable vision of the Godhead is reserved until eternal life for the pure of heart, the disciples could not, in their mortal flesh, look upon His glory. The Lord displayed His glory, there-

Reflections from the Fathers: Pope St. Leo the Great is an adaptation of selections from Sermon 51, "A Homily Delivered on the Saturday before the Second Sunday in Lent—On the Transfiguration," in *Nicene and Post-Nicene Fathers*, 2nd ser., vol. 12; available from www.ccel.org. Adapted from the 1888 edition, Christian Literature Publishing.

fore, to these three chosen witnesses, investing His body, which He has in common with all men, with such splendor. His face was like the sun's brightness, and His garments were like the whiteness of snow.

And in this Transfiguration the foremost object was to remove the offense of the Cross from the disciples' heart, and, by revealing to them the excellence of His hidden dignity, to prevent their faith from being disturbed by the humiliation of His voluntary Passion. And with no less foresight, the foundation was laid for the hope of the Holy Church that the whole Body of Christ might recognize the transformation that she would receive, and that her members would receive a share in that honor, which had already shone forth in their Head. The Lord Himself, when He spoke of the majesty of His coming, said: "Then the righteous will shine like the sun in the kingdom of their Father" (Mt. 13:43). The blessed Apostle Paul bears witness to the self-same thing, saying: "I consider that the sufferings of this present time are not worth comparing with the glory that is to be revealed to us" (Rom. 8:18). And again: "For you have died, and your life is hid with Christ in God. When Christ who is our life appears, then you also will appear with him in glory" (Col. 3:3–4). But to confirm the apostles and assist them in knowledge, additional instruction was conveyed by this miracle.

Moses and Elijah, that is the Law and the Prophets, appeared and talked with the Lord, that in the presence of those five men what had been said might be truly fulfilled: "[O]nly on the evidence of two witnesses, or of three witnesses, shall a charge be sustained" (Deut. 19:15). What could be more certain in this world than a proclamation joined by the trumpet of the Old and of the New Testament, and the documentary evidence of the ancient witnesses, combined with the teaching of the Gospel? For the pages of both covenants corroborate each other. He who under the veil of mysteries had been promised by signs that went before is clearly and conspicuously revealed by the splendor of the present glory. As the blessed John says, "[T]he law was given through Moses; grace and truth came through Jesus Christ" (Jn. 1:17). In Him is fulfilled both the promise of prophetic figures and the purpose of the Law, for He teaches the truth of prophecy by His presence, and renders the keeping of the commands possible through grace.

The Apostle Peter, being excited by the revelation of these mysteries, and despising things mundane and scorning things earthly, was seized with a sort of ecstatic longing for the things eternal. Being filled with rapture at the whole vision, He desired to make his abode with Jesus in the place where he had been blessed with the manifestation of His glory. And so Peter says, "Lord, it is well that we are here; if you wish, I will make three booths here, one for you and one for Moses and one for Elijah" (Mt. 17:4). But to this proposal the Lord made no answer, thereby signifying that what Peter wanted, although not evil, was contrary to the divine order—since the world could only be saved through Christ's death. By the Lord's example, the faithful were called upon to believe that, although we should not doubt the promises of happiness, we should understand that in the trials of this life we must ask for the power of endurance rather than for glory. The joyousness of reigning cannot precede the times of suffering.

And so, while Jesus was speaking, a bright cloud over-shadowed them, and a voice out of the cloud proclaimed, "This is my beloved Son, with whom I am well pleased; listen to Him" (Mt. 17:5). The Father was indeed present in the Son, and in the Lord's brightness, which was tempered for the disciples' sight. The Father's essence was not separated from the only begotten Son; but, in order to emphasize the two-fold personality, they saw the brilliance of the Son's body, and they heard the Father's voice from out of the cloud. And when this voice was heard, the disciples "fell on their faces, and were filled with awe" (Mt. 17:6), trembling at the majesty, not only of the Father, but also of the Son, for they now had a deeper insight into the undivided Deity of both. Even in their fear, they did not separate the One from the Other, because they doubted not in their faith. This was a profound testimony, containing a meaning deeper than words. For when the Father said, "This is my beloved Son," clearly He meant: "This is My Son, who is eternally from Me and with Me. The Begetter is not before the Begotten, nor does the Begotten come after the Begetter. This is My Son, who is separated from Me, neither by Godhead, nor by power, nor by eternity. This is My Son, not adopted, but true-born, not created from another source, but begotten of Me. He was not made like Me from another nature, but was born equal to Me of My nature. 'This is My Son,' through Whom 'all things were made . . . and without him was not anything made that was made' (Jn. 1:3). All things that I do, He does in like manner; and whatever I perform, He performs with Me inseparably and without difference. For the Son is in the Father and the Father in the Son, and

Our Unity is never divided. And though I am One who
begot, and He the Other whom I begot, it is yet wrong for
you to think anything of Him that is not possible of Me.
This is My Son, who sought not by grasping, and seized
nothing in greediness. He has equality with Me, but,
remaining in the form of My glory, and in order that He
might carry out Our common plan for the restoration of
mankind, He lowered the unchangeable Godhead even to
the form of a slave" (cf. Jn. 1:3; Jn. 10:38; Phil. 2:6).

"Listen to Him unhesitatingly, for in Him I am well
pleased. By His preaching I am manifested; by His humiliation I am glorified. He is the truth and the life; He is My
power and wisdom (cf. Jn. 14:6; 1 Cor. 1:24). Listen to
Him, whom the mysteries of the Law have foretold, whom
the mouths of prophets have sung. Listen to Him: He
redeems the world by His blood, He binds the devil, and
He carries off His chattels. He destroys the bond of sin
and the strangle hold of transgression. Listen to Him: He
opens the way to heaven, and by the punishment of the
Cross, He prepares for you the steps of ascent into the
Kingdom. Why do you tremble at being redeemed? Why
do you fear to be healed of your wounds? Be open to what
Christ and I desire. Cast away all fleshly fear and arm
yourselves with faithful constancy, for it is unworthy that
you should fear in the Savior's Passion what, by His good
gift, you shall not have to fear even at your own end."

Dearly beloved, these things were not said only for the
profit of the three apostles on the mountain, but for the
profit of the whole Church. Let all men's faith be strengthened by the preaching of the most holy Gospel, and let no
one be ashamed of Christ's Cross, through which the world

was redeemed. And let no one fear to suffer for righteousness' sake, or doubt the fulfillment of the promises, for this reason: that through toil, we pass to rest and, through death, to life. Christ assumed all the weakness of our humanity. If we abide in trust and love of Him, we conquer as He conquered and receive what He promised. Whether in the performance of His commands or in the endurance of adversities, the Father's voice should always be sounding in our ears, saying, "This is my beloved Son, with whom I am well pleased; listen to him," who lives and reigns with the Father and the Holy Spirit, forever and ever. Amen.

The Institution of the Eucharist

A final mystery of light is the institution of the Eucharist, in which Christ offers his body and blood as food under the signs of bread and wine, and testifies "to the end" his love for humanity (Jn. 13:1), for whose salvation he will offer himself in sacrifice.

—*John Paul II,* Rosarium Virginis Mariae

The Sacramental Expression of the Paschal Mystery

Now the feast of Unleavened Bread drew near, which is called the Passover. . . . And when the hour came, he sat at table, and the apostles with him. And he said to them, "I have earnestly desired to eat this passover with you before I suffer; for I tell you I shall not eat it until it is fulfilled in the kingdom of God." . . . And he took bread, and when he had given thanks he broke it and gave it to them, saying, "This is my body which is given for you. Do this in remembrance of me." And likewise the cup after supper, saying, "This cup which is poured out for you is the new covenant in my blood." (Lk. 22:1, 14–16, 19–20)[1]

During His entire ministry, Jesus continually gave of Himself—healing, teaching, and preaching, often when He was tired and in need of rest. At the Passover meal, when He institutes the Holy Eucharist, Jesus not only gives *of* Himself, but He gives *His very Self.* Christ's gift of the Eucharist teaches us about what is at the heart of His

---

[1] See also Mt. 26:26–28; Mk. 14:22–24; Jn. 13:7; Jn. 13–17 (John's account of what happens at the Last Supper and the prayer of Jesus). See also 1 Cor. 11:23–26; 1 Cor. 5:7; 1 Pet. 1:18–19.

divine life, an eternal gift of self in thanksgiving and love to the Father. God calls us to imitate His Son and, in remembrance of His awesome gift, to proclaim His mighty deeds by uniting the sacrifice of our lives to that of Christ's on the altar.

"Now the Feast of Unleavened Bread Drew Near"

At the climax of Jesus' ministry He comes to Jerusalem to celebrate the Passover with His apostles because "the feast of Unleavened Bread drew near" (Lk. 22:1). The prophets of Israel always did highly symbolic things at highly symbolic times, in order to communicate significant truths to the people of God. Jesus is no different. He chose the Passover as the context for His climatic closing actions. The time was now right for Jesus to give His greatest gift to the Church.

The first Passover celebrated the liberation of the nation of Israel from the rule and tyranny of the Egyptians. Every year when the Passover was celebrated, it recalled God's powerful salvation and looked forward to the day when Israel would be free from all oppression. At Jesus' time, Israel was living under the pagan rule of the Romans—and the need and desire for freedom was as thick in the air as smoke after Fourth of July fireworks.

Put yourself in Peter and John's sandals. Peter had identified that Jesus was the Messiah and the Chosen One of God, and both he and John believed that this was true. Jesus had been transfigured in their very presence. And now they were asked by Jesus to prepare a room for the Passover (Lk. 22:8). What were these two disciples thinking about this night? Traditionally, whenever the Passover was celebrated, the youngest at table would ask the host, "Why is this night different from all other nights?" This question must have been on the minds and hearts of all the apostles gathered together with Him at the meal. They may have been eager with anticipation—was tonight going to be the night that Jesus would reveal Himself? Perhaps they felt that something incredible was about to happen; perhaps Jesus was about to free Israel from the rule of the Romans.

"I Have Earnestly Desired to Eat This Passover with You before I Suffer"

Jesus knew that this night was different from all others. The events that were about to unfold were part of His plan from the beginning: "And when the hour came, he sat at table, and the apostles with him. And he said to them, 'I have earnestly desired to eat this passover with you before I suffer'" (Lk. 22:14–15). Following the Passover tradition, this "hour" mentioned by Luke begins the Passover meal in the evening, just as the Israelites in Egypt had celebrated it "in the evening" (Ex. 12:6). At the meal, the host, surrounded by family and friends, would retell the story of Israel's redemption as those present ate unleavened bread, drank cups of wine, and consumed the paschal lamb. Jesus follows the Jewish tradition and ritual meal, but changes the words and prayers to give it new meaning: "[B]y celebrating the Last Supper with his apostles in the course of the Passover meal, Jesus gave the Jewish Passover its definitive meaning" (*Catechism*, no. 1340).

What meaning is Jesus trying to convey as He dines with His apostles? "And he took bread, and when he had given thanks he broke it and gave it to them, saying, 'This is my body which is given for you. Do this in remembrance of me.' And likewise the cup after supper, saying, 'This cup which is poured out for you is the new covenant in my blood'" (Lk. 22:19–20). When we look at this Scripture passage, we can see that it refers to a meal—a meal of bread and wine. Jesus' words signal to us that He is giving the meal a new significance. He does not use the words, "Take this bread for your nourishment, and take this wine for your drink." In the very words of the institution of the Eucharist, "This is my body which is given for you," Jesus combines the significance of the meal with that of a sacrifice—the sacrifice of Good Friday. Jesus breaks the bread as a symbol of what will happen to His body. His body will be beaten, scourged, crowned with thorns, and broken during the Passion. In the same way, Jesus takes the cup of wine, blesses it, and gives it to His apostles as a sign of His blood being poured out and spilled during the Passion "for the forgiveness of sins" (Mt. 26:28). With Jesus' words, the bread becomes His Body, and the wine becomes His Blood.

One of the key elements of the Passover meal was the sacrificed lamb. Luke even mentions this point: "Then came the day of Unleavened Bread, on which the Passover lamb had to be sacrificed" (Lk. 22:7). At the original Passover, the angel of death "passed over" the houses that had the blood of the sacrificial lamb smeared on the doorpost. It was the blood of the lamb that saved the Israelites from the plague that killed all the Egyptian first-born sons. At the Last Supper, no lamb is mentioned. All of the Gospel writers fail to mention a lamb being present. Why does one of the key elements of the Passover meal seem to be missing? Because the true Lamb of sacrifice was the host of this meal. Jesus and His blood would be the saving factors of the New Passover. Saint Peter reflects on this truth when he writes: "You know that you were ransomed from the futile ways inherited from your fathers, not with perishable things such as silver or gold, but with the precious blood of Christ, like that of a lamb without blemish or spot" (1 Pet. 1:18–19). Saint Paul also tells us, "for Christ our paschal lamb, has been sacrificed" (1 Cor. 5:7).

In addition to sacrificing the lamb, the Israelites were commanded to eat it: "They shall eat the flesh that night" (Ex. 12:8). Eating the lamb was an essential part of the sacrifice. In fact, eating the sacrifice actually brought about the saving action of God. In both the old Passover of the Jews and the New Passover of Jesus, the meal is the sacrifice. The *Catechism* teaches that the altar of sacrifice is also the table of the Lord. The victim and the food are one and the same (cf. no. 1383).

"The New Covenant in My Blood"

One of the most crucial and important themes of Scripture is that of covenants. God communicated most intimately with His people through establishing covenants. Covenants create family bonds. They often consist of signs related to blood, because they extend blood relations. Think of Tom Sawyer and Huckleberry Finn. They believe that they are not only friends, but also brothers—and so they each make a cut on their arms and mix their blood in order to signify, as covenants do, a familial bond. Think of marriage. Two separate individuals from different families and backgrounds come together and "covenant" themselves to each other. Now, they are one, and they have brought their whole family with them. Covenants, then, extend family bonds and relationships.

The covenant that God made with Israel through Moses was sealed by blood, signifying the new kinship between the two parties. The ceremony that ratified this covenant, which God made with Israel through Moses, is found in Exodus 24. After the sacrifices of oxen, half of the blood is put into basins, and half is thrown against the altar of the Lord. Moses reads the Law to the people, and they tell him they will be obedient to it: "And Moses took the blood and threw it upon the people, and said, 'Behold the blood of the covenant which the LORD has made with you in accordance with all these words'" (Ex. 24:8). This action of throwing blood on the altar and on the people signified God becoming one with the people through a covenant. Traditionally, sharing a meal sealed the covenant. This is the significance of the Passover meal shared by God and the people of Israel at the end of the ceremony (cf. Ex. 24:11).

All this should give us new insight into the Last Supper. The first time that Jesus uses the word "covenant" is at the Last Supper—His Passover. Jesus forges a new and everlasting covenant with His people in His blood. He gives Himself to His people in an intimate and real relationship. By giving us His Body and Blood, Christ constitutes us into His family. Just as sharing the same blood makes a group of individuals a family, so now through the Body and Blood of Christ we are the family of God. When Moses threw blood on the people at the covenant ceremony, it was only an external sign that there was a union between God and man. At Jesus' Passover, we actually share in covenant with God in a whole new way, because it is Jesus, the Son of God, who gives us His blood. The Old Covenant and Passover liberated the nation of Israel from the bondage of slavery in Egypt. The New Covenant of Jesus' blood saves and liberates all people from the true slavery of sin. But the good news does not end there. It not only saves us from sin; it also sets us apart for sonship in Christ.

"And When He Had Given Thanks"

One of the names the early Christians gave the sacrament of the Last Supper is Holy "Eucharist." This is a Greek word that means "thanksgiving." Luke tells us: "And he took bread, and when he had given *thanks* he broke it and gave it to them" (22:19). In the Greek text it would read, "when he had given *eucharistia*." A prayer of thanksgiving is at the very core of the meaning of the bread being broken and the wine being poured out. The *Catechism of the Catholic Church* reflects on the Eucharist: "We must therefore consider the Eucharist as: thanksgiving and praise to the *Father*; the sacrificial memorial of *Christ* and his Body; the presence of Christ by the power of his word and of his *Spirit*" (*Catechism*, no. 1358, emphasis in original). In the life of the Trinity, Jesus eternally makes a gift of Himself back to the Father, in thanksgiving for the Father's love. Christ's self-sacrifice of love, on the Cross and in the institution of the Eucharist, is a continuation on earth of His divine life in heaven.

Thanksgiving is intrinsic to the name and meaning of the sacrament Christ left us. What are we thankful for?

Like Christ, we offer our prayer of thanksgiving to the person of the Father. On behalf of all creation, the Church offers the Eucharistic sacrifice to the Father. Everything "good, beautiful, and just in creation and in humanity" (*Catechism*, no. 1359), which the Father has created, is offered back to Him through Christ and in the power of the Holy Spirit.

The next time you are at Mass, pay close attention to the preparation of the gifts. Someone usually brings up the bread and wine to be used at the celebration on behalf of the whole Church. The priest addresses this prayer over the bread and wine to the Father: "Blessed are you, Lord, God of all creation. Through your goodness we have this bread to offer, which earth has given and human hands have made. It will become for us the bread of life." And then: "Blessed are you, Lord, God of all creation. Through your goodness we have this wine to offer, fruit of the vine and work of human hands. It will become our spiritual drink."[2] The Eucharist is a prayer of thanksgiving to God the Father for all the goodness He has given us—most especially, for having given us His Son.

"Do This in Remembrance of Me"

At the institution of the first Passover, the Lord commanded the people of Israel, "This day shall be for you a *memorial* day, and you shall keep it as a feast to the LORD" (Ex. 12:14). The *Catechism* tells us: "In the sense of Sacred Scripture the *memorial* is not merely the recollection of

---

[2] The Liturgy of the Eucharist, *Sacramentary*, 371.

past events but the proclamation of the mighty works wrought by God for men [cf. Ex. 13:3]" (no. 1363, emphasis added). Year after year at the Passover, the Israelites recalled and proclaimed the mighty works God had done for them in the Exodus. In doing so, those events were made present to them once again, and they *remembered and relived* the actual Exodus event. Likewise, the Church at each and every Eucharist recalls and proclaims the great work of redemption that God has accomplished in the person of Jesus Christ. When the Church prays the words of institution of the Eucharist in the liturgy of the Mass, this actually makes present the saving actions of Christ. The Eucharist is the sacrificial memorial of Christ and His Body, the Church.

Jesus commands the apostles at the New Passover, "Do this in *remembrance* of me." After the priest says these words in the Mass—"Do this in memory of me"—a prayer called the *anamnesis* is said. We celebrate Jesus, now present under the appearance of bread and wine, and recall the memorial of Christ. "Father, we celebrate the *memory* of Christ, your Son (Eucharistic Prayer I). "In *memory* of his death and resurrection . . ." (Eucharistic Prayer II). "Father, *calling to mind* the death your Son endured for our salvation . . ." (Eucharistic Prayer III). "Father, we now celebrate this *memorial* of our redemption" (Eucharistic Prayer IV).[3] Each Eucharistic prayer recalls the memory of Christ's sacrificial meal by making it present in the biblical sense.

---

[3] *Sacramentary*, 546, 550, 554, 559, emphasis added.

"This Is My Body, This Is My Blood"

When the priest utters the words, "This is my Body," and, "This is my Blood," he does so *in persona Christi*, in the person of Christ. With their utterance, Christ becomes present on the altar in the Eucharistic species. The Second Vatican Council mentions the many ways that Jesus is present in His Church: in the proclaimed word of Scripture, where two or three are gathered in His name; in the minister; in the sacraments; and in the Mass. But, above all the others, the Council proclaims, "[H]e is present . . . most *especially in the Eucharistic species [SC 7]*." Jesus becomes "*truly, really, and substantially*" present—Body, Blood, Soul, and Divinity—in the Eucharist (*Catechism*, no. 1373, 1374, emphasis in original).

This is accomplished by the power of Christ's word and the Holy Spirit. The power of the Holy Spirit comes and makes good the words of Christ concerning the Eucharist. At the offertory of the Mass, the gifts of bread and wine are brought forward on behalf of all the members of the Church. The priest, in the person of Christ, speaking the words of Christ, then offers the bread and wine to God the Father. In turn, by the power of the Holy Spirit, bread and wine are changed into the Body and Blood of Jesus. Christ wanted to leave a sign of His love and His presence among us. He chose to do so under the humble appearances of bread and wine.

Bread and wine are incredible symbols of the Christian life. Bread is made with many grains of wheat gathered together. They are then broken, ground, and shaped into loaves. When the dough is placed in the oven, it is baked at high temperatures before it is ready to eat. Wine is made with grapes, gathered and plucked off a vine, which are then crushed and mashed until every bit of juice is squeezed out of them. Finally, they are left in barrels for a long time until they ferment and become wine.

Much like the individual grains and grapes, the Church is composed of many members that become one Body in Christ (1 Cor. 12:12). In trying to follow Christ and imitate Him, much of our old life must be broken and crushed. We can be "baked" at a high temperature through the trials and the temptations that we face, and these hardships and sufferings can sometimes last a long time. Saint Paul tells the Romans (and us), "I appeal to you therefore, brethren, by the mercies of God, to present your bodies as a living sacrifice, holy and acceptable to God, which is your spiritual worship" (Rom. 12:1). The greatest spiritual sacrifice and worship we can offer is our very lives. In the Old Covenant, the sacrifices of bulls and sheep offered to God were dead for good reason— live animals would hardly submit to such treatment willingly. But God asks something more of each one of us— to be a living sacrifice and to *willingly* offer ourselves as a sacrifice to Him.

The *Catechism* teaches: "In the Eucharist the sacrifice of Christ becomes also the sacrifice of the members of his Body. The lives of the faithful, their praise, sufferings, prayer, and work, are united with those of Christ and with his total offering, and so acquire a new value. Christ's sacrifice present on the altar makes it possible for all generations of Christians to be united with his offering" (no. 1368). When the priest offers the bread and wine to God the Father, he is offering us up to the Father along with Christ. Your life can be transformed when it is placed on the altar at Mass. Put all your troubles on the altar: any hurtful actions or comments directed against you, the business deal that fell through, your child's sickness, the blessings you have received, the prayers on your heart, etc. Put everything in your life on the altar to be transformed by Christ and given to the Father at the consecration of every Mass that you attend.

Amazement and Invitation

Pope John Paul II gave the Church a great gift in his encyclical on the Eucharist, *Ecclesia de Eucharistia.* One of the reasons he wrote it was to "rekindle Eucharistic 'amazement.'"[4] We should marvel at the gift of Jesus present in the Eucharistic bread and wine: "In this gift Jesus Christ entrusted to His Church the perennial making present of the paschal mystery. . . . The thought of this leads us to profound amazement and gratitude. . . . This amazement should always fill the Church assembled for the celebration of the Eucharist" (*EE* 5). When we approach the celebration of the Mass, whether it be at a splendid Easter Mass or a Sunday Mass or a simple daily Mass, we should be filled with amazement at the wonderful gift Jesus has given us.

This amazement at the Eucharist will lead us to adore Jesus more profoundly in the Blessed Sacrament. Throughout the day or week, we should prepare to receive

---

[4] Pope John Paul II, Encyclical Letter on the Eucharist in Its Relationship to the Church *Ecclesia de Eucharistia* (April 17, 2003), no. 6 (hereafter cited in the text as *EE*).

Him in Holy Communion. There was once a monk who, whenever he was asked what he was doing, whether it was trimming the hedges, doing the dishes, or making dinner, would reply, "I am preparing for Mass." His attitude and life was completely centered on the Eucharist in constant adoration. The more you adore, the greater your desire will be for Holy Communion. "Communion" reminds us of two English words, "common" and "union." We share a common union with others, in that we receive the same Lord; but most especially, we find union with Christ, because it is He whom we receive.

Pope John Paul II has frequently encouraged adoration of the Blessed Sacrament. Even if we cannot give a full hour each day in prayer, we can carve out something for God. The Pope comments: "The Church and the world have a great need of eucharistic worship. Jesus waits for us in this sacrament of love. Let us be generous with our time in going to meet Him in adoration, and in contemplation that is full of faith, and ready to make reparation for the great faults and crimes of the world by our adoration, never cease."[5]

* * * *

*Let us pray for the fruit of a
deeper reverence of the Eucharist.*

We pray that we may offer our lives to God in a constant attitude of "thanksgiving," mindful of all the blessings God has bestowed on us, the greatest being the very gift

---

[5] Pope John Paul II, Letter on the Mystery and the Worship of the Eucharist *Dominicae Cenae* (February 24, 1980), no. 3.

of His Son in the Eucharist. May this lead to a profound gratitude, deeper praise, and continual thanksgiving to God, made manifest through our reverence for the Eucharist. Amen.

Points for Reflection

1. The first Passover brought liberation and freedom to the Israelites from the slavery imposed by the Egyptians. At the time of Jesus, the Israelites were awaiting a new exodus more powerful than the first (cf. Is. 52). Many of them thought it was to be a political liberation from the Romans. Instead, Jesus came to free us from our true enemy—Satan and sin. What does it feel like to be a slave? Sin shackles us and prevents us from following Christ. Are there any sins that are binding you and preventing you from imitating Christ? Do you live like you have been saved from sin?

2. It was the blood of the lamb smeared on the wooden doorposts that saved the Israelites from the angel of death. It is the blood of the true Paschal Lamb, Jesus, smeared on the wood of the Cross that is our entry into heaven. Do you see the Cross in your life as a real way to enter on the path that leads you to heaven?

3. In the first Exodus, the eating of the sacrificed lamb brought about salvation by God. In the New Exodus, when we eat the Body and Blood of Christ, we participate in the sacrifice of the Cross. This action actually brings about our salvation. In fact, it is a command by Jesus, "[U]nless you eat the flesh of the Son of man and

drink his blood, you have no life in you; he who eats my flesh and drinks my blood has eternal life, and I will raise him up at the last day" (Jn. 6:53–54). Do you see your reception of the Eucharist as applying the fruits of the Cross to your daily life?

4. Recent polls taken by secular papers of Catholics' belief in the Eucharist have shown that the majority either does not believe in or misunderstands the Real Presence. Do you believe Jesus is present like He promised? How can you increase your belief in the Real Presence?

5. At the very heart of the meaning of the Eucharist is thanksgiving. Thanksgiving should be a habitual way of life for us (cf. Col. 3:17). During the offertory, we thank God for His goodness. How have you seen God's goodness in your life and in the lives of others? What are you thankful for—family, friends, faith, talents, education, career opportunities, etc.? Do you tell the Creator and Giver of these gifts, "Thank You"?

6. When you pray, do you "remember" by placing yourself in the scenes on which you meditate? Do you ask Mary to help you? Do you have any memories or remembrances from a time when you were really touched by Jesus in the Eucharist? The Eucharist is not supposed to be just a recalling of past events, but a real "proclamation of the mighty works wrought by God for men" (*Catechism*, no. 1363). What mighty works has God done for you? How do you proclaim it?

7. It is so easy to "go through the motions" when it comes to attending Church. Next time you genuflect or reverence the Eucharist, think about what you are doing with your body. What kind of message are you sending out to people who may be watching? What kind of message are you sending to God?

Saint John Chrysostom

Now as they were eating, Jesus took bread, and blessed, and broke it, and gave it to the disciples and said, "Take, eat; this is my body." And he took a cup, and when he had given thanks he gave it to them, saying, "Drink of it, all of you; for this is my blood of the covenant, which is poured out for many for the forgiveness of sins. (Mt. 26:26–28)

"Now as they were eating, Jesus took bread, and blessed, and broke it." Why did Jesus establish this sacrament at the time of the Passover? He did it so that you would learn both that He is the lawgiver of the Old Testament, and that the events of the Old Testament foreshadow those in the New Covenant. We learn the truth of the New by examining the Old.

"Reflections from the Fathers: Saint John Chrysostom" is an adaptation of selections from Homily 82, from "Homilies on the Gospel of St. Matthew," in *Nicene and Post-Nicene Fathers*, 1st ser., vol. 10; available from www.ccel.org. Adapted from the 1888 edition, Christian Literature Publishing.

The Last Supper, then, is a sure sign of the fullness of times, when the old passes away and the things that were now come to an end.

At that Supper, Jesus gives thanks, to teach us how we should celebrate this sacrament, to show us that He came to the Passion willingly, and in this teaches us that, whatever we suffer, we should endure. In imitating Christ, we find hope, even in the midst of suffering. If, in the Old Testament, Passover brought deliverance from slavery, how much more will the truth of Jesus in the Eucharist set the world free and deliver His people! Therefore, I would add that, by establishing this feast of the New Covenant, the feast of the Old Covenant ceases. Passover, the primary feast of the Old Covenant, is replaced by one of far greater value. As Jesus says, "Take and eat. *This is My body*, which is broken for many."

And why are the apostles able to understand these words of Jesus? Because He had previously told them many things that alluded to this New Covenant. Jesus now speaks of the reason for His Passion, namely, the taking away of sins. He sheds His blood to establish a New Testament—a new beginning, a new promise, and a new law. As the Old Testament had sheep and bullocks for sacrifice, so the New has the Lord's blood. Jesus shows the apostles that He is soon to die and thus establish a New Covenant; at the same time, He reminds them of the former covenant, which also was established with the shedding of blood. He tells His disciples the reason for His death, the sacrifice of His blood, "which is poured out for many for the forgiveness of sins." And He says, "Do this in remembrance of me" (Lk. 22:19). Note how

He moves away from Jewish customs. With these words, Jesus is telling the apostles: As you celebrated the Passover in remembrance of the miracles in Egypt, so now do this likewise in remembrance of Me. The blood of the Passover lamb was shed for the preservation of the first-born; the blood of Christ is shed for the remission of the sins of the whole world. "[F]or this," He says, "is my blood . . . which is poured out for the many for the for-giveness of sins"

Jesus speaks these words both to indicate that His Passion and Cross are a mystery and also to comfort His disciples. As Moses said, "This day shall be for you a memorial day" (Ex. 12:14); so too, Jesus says, "[A]s often as you eat this bread and drink the cup, you proclaim the Lord's death until he comes" (1 Cor. 11:26). He also tells the apostles, "I have earnestly desired to eat this Passover with you" (Lk. 22:15); that is, to give to you the rites of a New Passover.

In this sacrament, Jesus identifies the memorial of this meal with His death, and by so doing silences heretics. For later, when they ask where it is manifest that Christ was sacrificed, we counter that if Jesus did not die, what is it that the rites symbolize?

Christ continually reminds us of the Passion through the sacrament (so that no man should be deceived). Christ both saves and teaches by means of that sacred table. Of all the Lord's blessings, this sacrament is preeminent, as Paul often emphasizes.

Then Jesus says, "I tell you I shall not drink again of the fruit of the vine until that day when I drink it new with you in my Father's kingdom" (Mt. 26:29). As He had spoken of His Passion and Cross, He now speaks of His Resurrection. Why then did Christ drink again with His disciples after His Resurrection? He does so lest the ignorant suppose that the Resurrection was only an appearance—for the doubting needed this as an infallible sign of His having risen again. In this way the apostles could bear witness to the Resurrection, saying, "[W]e . . . ate and drank with Him" (Acts 10:41).

To show therefore that they would see Him risen again, that He would be with them once more, and that they themselves would be witnesses to the things that are done, both by sight and by act, He said, "Until that day when I drink it new with you, you will bear witness, for you shall see Me risen again."

But what does Christ mean by "new"? On that day, after the Resurrection, Jesus will indeed "drink it new," for He will have an immortal and incorruptible body, which does not need food. So then it was not because of hunger that He ate and drank after the Resurrection, for His body did not need these things any more. He did it as a proof of His Resurrection.

*****

Let us then believe God in everything and never contradict Him, even if it should seem contrary to our thoughts and senses—let His word be of higher authority than our reason or sight. Thus let us accept the reality of the Eucharist, not looking at the things set before us, but keeping in mind Christ's words.

For His word cannot deceive, but our senses are easily beguiled. Since then the Word says, "This is my body," let us be persuaded and believe, looking at it with the eyes of the mind.

How many now say: "I wish that I could see His form, His clothes, His shoes"? But you do see Him, you do touch Him; you eat Him! You desire to see His clothes, but He gives Himself not only for you to see, but also to touch and eat and receive within you.

Therefore let no one approach the Eucharist with indifference. Be not faint-hearted, but come with burning hearts, fervent and roused. For if Jews at the Passover stood with their shoes on and their staffs in their hands, eating with haste, how much more should you be watchful! They were going to Palestine, wearing the garb of pilgrims; but you are about to approach heaven.

It is necessary therefore to be vigilant in all respects, for no small punishment is appointed to those who partake of the Eucharist unworthily.

Consider how indignant you are against the traitor Judas, and against those who crucified Christ. Watch, then, lest you also become guilty of betraying the Body and Blood of Christ. They slaughtered the all-holy body; but will you receive it into a filthy soul? It was not enough for Christ to become man and to be smitten and slaughtered, but He also chose to commingle Himself with us, not only by faith, but also by making us His very Body. Consider what an honor this is, and from what sort of table you are partaking. Even the angels tremble upon beholding this table, and dare not so much as look up at it without awe, because such brightness shines from it. With this we are fed, with this we are commingled, and we are made one body and one flesh with Christ. "Who can utter the mighty doings of the LORD, or show forth all his praise?" (cf. Psalms 106:2). What shepherd feeds His sheep with His own limbs? There are often mothers who, after the labor of birth, send their children to be nursed by other women; Christ does not do this, but rather feeds us with His own blood and, by this means, binds us to Himself.

Let us not then be remiss, for we have been counted worthy of so much love and honor. Do you not see with what eagerness the infants lay hold of the breast? With what earnest desire they fix their lips upon the nipple? With much more eagerness let us, as infants at the breast, approach the Eucharistic table and draw out the grace of the Spirit. Let it be our one sorrow, not to partake of this spiritual food. This sacrament set before us is not of man's power. The same Christ who established the Eucharist at the Last Supper also continues His work now. So let no Judas be present, no covetous man. If any one is not a disciple, let him withdraw, for the table is not for such. For "I keep the Passover," He said, "with My disciples."

I speak not only to the communicant, but also I say to the priest who ministers the sacrament: distribute this Gift with much care. There is no small punishment for you, if being conscious of any wickedness in any man, you allow him to partake of the banquet of the table. "[S]hall I not now require his blood at your hand?" (2 Sam. 4:11). If some public figure, or some wealthy person who is unworthy, presents himself to receive Holy Communion, forbid him. The authority that you have is greater than his. Consider if your task were to guard a clean spring of water for a flock, and you saw a sheep approach with mire on its mouth—you would not allow it to stoop down and pollute the stream. You are now entrusted with a spring, not of water, but of blood and of spirit. If you see someone having sin in his heart (which is far more grievous than earth and mire), coming to receive the Eucharist, are you not concerned? Do you not try to prevent him? What excuse can you have, if you do not?

God has honored you with the dignity of priesthood, that you might discern these things. This is not to say that you should go about clothed in a white and shining vestment; but this is your office; this, your safety; this, your whole crown.

You ask how you should know which individual is unworthy to receive? I am speaking here not of some unknown sinner, but of a notorious one.

If someone who is not a disciple, through ignorance, comes to Communion, do not be afraid to forbid him. Fear God, not man. If you fear man, you will be scorned and laughed at even by him; but if you fear God, you will be an object of respect even to men.

But if you cannot do it, bring that sinner to me, for I will not allow anyone to dare do these things. I would give up my life rather than give the Lord's blood to the unworthy.

If, however, a sinful person receives Communion and you did not know his character, you are not to blame. I say the things above concerning only those who sin openly. For if we amend these, God will speedily reveal to us the unknown also; but if we let these flagrant abuses continue, how can we expect Him to make manifest those that are hidden? I say these things, not to repel sinners or cut them off, but I say it in order that we may bring them to repentance, and bring them back, so that we may take care of them. For thus we shall both please God and lead many to receive worthily. And for our own diligence, and for our care for others, we will receive a great reward. May we attain that reward by the grace and love that God gives to man through our Lord Jesus Christ, to whom be glory, world without end. Amen.